PUBLIC DIMENSIONS
OF A BELIEVER'S LIFE

PUBLIC DIMENSIONS OF A BELIEVER'S LIFE

Rediscovering the Cardinal Virtues

Monika K. Hellwig

ROWMAN & LITTLEFIELD PUBLISHERS, INC
Lanham • Boulder • New York • Toronto • Oxford

ROWMAN & LITTLEFIELD PUBLISHERS, INC.

Published in the United States of America
by Rowman & Littlefield Publishers, Inc.
A wholly owned subsidiary of The Rowman & Littlefield Publishing Group, Inc.
4501 Forbes Boulevard, Suite 200, Lanham, Maryland 20706
www.rowmanlittlefield.com

PO Box 317
Oxford
OX2 9RU, UK

British Library Cataloguing in Publication Information Available

Library of Congress Cataloging-in-Publication Data

Hellwig, Monika.
  Public dimensions of a believer's life : rediscovering the cardinal virtues /
Monika K. Hellwig.
     p. cm.
  Includes index.
  ISBN 0-7425-5014-1 (cloth : alk. paper)—ISBN 0-7425-5015-X (pbk. :
alk. paper)
  1. Christian ethics—Catholic authors. 2. Cardinal virtues. 3. Social ethics.
I. Title.
  BJ1249.H519 2005
  241'.4—dc22   2005013885

Printed in the United States of America

∞™ The paper used in this publication meets the minimum requirements of
American National Standard for Information Sciences—Permanence of Paper
for Printed Library Materials, ANSI/NISO Z39.48-1992.

This work is dedicated to the memory of
Frank Sheed & Maisie Ward
who spent their lives bringing out of the
Christian storehouse treasures both old and new.

CONTENTS

Contents

ACKNOWLEDGMENTS

All those whom I have known in the course of a lifetime have contributed in some way to this book.

Chapters 1 and 2, like much else in the book, are especially indebted to all that I have learned of Ignatian spirituality from many good mentors, both in the United States and earlier in my life in Britain and Rome.

Chapters 3 and 9 are heavily indebted to a presentation made by Professor Dan Finn of St. John's University, Collegeville, Minnesota, at the 2003 Annual Convention of the Catholic Theological Society of America, where he reflected on the issues that came up for him in his volunteer work in community organizing of the underprivileged.

The encouragement of many friends, and especially of Jeremy Longford of Sheed & Ward, kept the project alive through the disruption of a house fire and a number of moves.

In spite of which, if there is aught here disedifying, misleading, or heretical, that is surely my original contribution.

Introduction

TENSIONS IN THE
DYNAMIC OF THE REDEMPTION

This book is about human responsibility in public life and the moral and spiritual factors involved in exercising that responsibility. It is not addressed to politicians as such but to ordinary citizens like myself. It does not aim to preach from a stance of certified and authoritative wisdom but to share insights, understanding, and continuing questions from the position of a fellow seeker. It is a book based on personal experience and reflection within the shared wisdom of the Catholic tradition. At the same time, it is based on the observation that massive changes in the world in the course of the twentieth century have left us with ever new and uncharted tasks in social responsibility. We must find paths through situations in which we have never been before.

This book, therefore, has been prompted by my own experiences and observations over a lifetime. That lifetime included Hitler's rise to power when I was a child in a partly Jewish, partly Christian family in Germany and the Netherlands. It also included the horrors of the Second World War when we school-age children, rescued from the ground war

on the European continent, were moved around Scotland
and England, separated from our parents and relatives, in
boarding schools and host families, to avoid the bombard-
ment as much as possible. In the following years, there was
the rebuilding of Europe and the collapse of the colonial
era around the world—Mahatma Gandhi's nonviolent Indian independence movement and the subsequent horribly
violent partition of India and Pakistan. There was the polarization of the Western and communist zones of influence and the Cold War. Then there was the Civil Rights
Movement with its martyrs in the United States and the
struggle against apartheid with its martyrs in South Africa.
This was followed, decade after decade, by terrible civil wars
and repeated famines sweeping the newly independent
countries of Africa. In the Catholic Church, there was the
Second Vatican Council, during which I was in Rome, followed by wave after wave both of change and of resistance
to change in the church. There had been the Korean War. It
was followed not much later by the Vietnam War. There
were upheavals and demonstrations in the United States
over the morality and prudence of the latter, in spite of
which the war, with its terrible toll of lives on both sides,
dragged on and on. Finally, there was Rwanda's civil war
while the world looked on, reluctant to intervene in the
massive slaughter.

Of course, not everything that happened in the world
during this lifetime was tragic, but much of it was monumental in the changes brought. In Latin America, and later
elsewhere in the Third World, there were the stirrings of liberation movements and conscientization of the poor and
oppressed, with Christian church authorities, theologians,
and activists ranged both in support and in opposition. In

the northern hemisphere, there was the peaceful collapse of the Soviet Empire from within, in the Far East the peaceful overthrow of the Philippine dictator, in Africa the peaceful ending of apartheid in the Union of South Africa. Each of these also had its martyrs. Some terrible regimes came to an end in Latin America, though elsewhere, as in El Salvador, Colombia, and Chiapas there have been once again martyrs, and desperate undocumented immigrants have been dying in the Arizona desert. In the United States, the Civil Rights movement blossomed into antidiscrimination efforts addressing the more subtle and elusive injustices, which is certainly progress toward a more humane society. At the same time, poverty, unemployment, and inadequate education among racial and ethnic minorities are high.

With the end of the Cold War between the capitalist and communist spheres of influence, the polarization has shifted rather than disappeared. Hostility of the West toward the Islamic countries has yielded the long-term tragedy of the Palestinians, a war against Afghanistan, two brutal and indecisive wars against Iraq, and a global web of terrorist activity. The world economy is troubled and fragile; AIDS is decimating large regions in Africa and elsewhere; the world refugee situation looks insoluble; support for the United Nations is uncertain; and peace-keepers in various parts of the world have a daunting task. In all of this, there have been and are many decisions to be made, not only by governments and international agencies, but by all of us. In democratic societies there are decisions for everyone whether to engage or isolate oneself, whether to support or oppose certain government actions, and whether and where to become personally involved in some way. In all societies there are some decisions that one cannot avoid—situations where not to decide is to decide by implication and without accepting responsibility—situations like the rise of Hitler to power in Germany, like the extension and later the crumbling of the Soviet Union, like the Indian Independence Movement, like the Civil Rights Movement, like the uprising of the Chiapas Indians.

None of the events named above simply happened to people. They were brought about by the actions of some and the inaction of others, by decisions that were wise and for the common good, and by other decisions that were made by people who were selfish, power-hungry, greedy, or frightened. Many decisions were probably made without much reflection, by taking much for granted, and yet they had momentous consequences for large numbers of people. There are some kinds of decisions one tends to take with little critical reflection; they are those that express the prevailing values of one's society. Decisions expressing counter-cultural values require more personal evaluation. Hence, natural lethargy, love of comfort, and need of routine and reassurance all weigh against taking a stance over against the prevailing values and expectations. But it is not only this. It is also a fact that the prevailing values and expectations are generally those that we are authoritatively taught are right and that are therefore very hard to question. It requires a certain level of human intellectual and affective maturity to think reflexively and critically about values and expectations of one's society that one has internalized as components of one's own character and identity. Besides personal maturity and critical independence in thought, one needs criteria outside the assumed and expected. When people stand out as courageous dissenters, it is often religious faith that has supplied the alternative criteria.

This book is about the decisions people have to make in human affairs at all levels of social organization. It is about the values that guide our decisions and about the way those values are often apparently in conflict with one another. There are, of course, conflicts in every life. They are of many kinds, including those tensions that are the interplay of moral values when these appear to conflict in practice. This book addresses especially such conflicts in a believer's life when they seem to be rooted in the very nature of the redemption as understood in Christian theology. Nevertheless, readers of other religious traditions may recognize parallels. The underlying human issues are experienced by all of us of whatever tradition, and each tradition has developed its own way of naming these issues and prescribing ways of dealing with them successfully.

In Western thought, this has largely been formulated in terms of moral virtues. The analysis of the various kinds of moral virtue required for a wholesome and integral human life goes back to ancient times. It passed into Christian tradition through the pagan Greek philosophers whose wisdom came to be treasured by Christian philosophers and theologians through the centuries. In the analysis of the ancient philosophers, the "cardinal virtues," those on which all aspects of behavior seem to "hinge," so to speak, are four. They are prudence, justice, fortitude, and temperance. These cardinal virtues are integral to the discussion throughout the book, but chapters 1 through 12 deal with practical issues and dilemmas that Christian believers have to confront in practice, in private and public life, in business and the professions, as citizens and as neighbors, in political and in economic matters, and so forth. It is only in the conclusion that you will find a more theoretical discussion of the cardinal virtues and the way they are modified when seen in the context of the Christian understanding of the redemption.

Yet some preliminary reflections are in order.

The Christian understanding of the good life grounds its logic centrally in the doctrine of the redemption. The world with its human affairs as we know them is not for a Christian believer the best of all possible worlds. Nor is it simply to be equated with the will or intent of the creator. All that exists is indeed the creation of a single, benign divine source that is revealed in its creation but remains mystery and transcendence. However, the creation is dynamic and continuing and brings forth with human collaboration whatever is incomplete. By its nature, the universe as created looks for development and completion from within its own resources.

At the heart of this process are the communities of human beings becoming conscious of the processes of the universe, trying to understand them, trying to shape and control them. People are equipped not only with intelligence and ability to learn but also with desires and the ability to achieve, relate, and control. Not everything that is possible works for the common well-being and harmony. Not everything that has actually been done by human beings has been pure benefit for the well-being and harmony of the creatures of the universe. We ourselves, and the world about us, inherit both blessing and curse from the creativity of those before us.

Yet, in the Christian vision of history, we are not simply condemned to make the best of things in an endless repetition of wars, famines, injustices, oppressions, prejudices, injuries, and sufferings of all kinds, spiraling ever more rapidly to global terrorism, mass destruction, and universal fear. The optimism that denies the inevitability of doom is based on the conviction of an initially good though unfinished creation not abandoned by its creator. In the Christian vision, evil and its reproductive power are very real, but so is the healing intervention of the divine in history. The historical person of Jesus of Nazareth is the focal point that gives meaning, perspective, and challenge to one's life and action in the world. The project of Jesus to which Christian believers are assimilated as active participants is the redemption of all creation from forces of destruction. The possibility of success is divinely guaranteed. Timetables for attaining the goals are not so guaranteed and depend on the freely chosen collaboration of human communities.

This clearly sets a frame of reference for what constitutes a good life. It is a frame of reference that is different from the one that gave rise to the classic Greek understanding of virtue. It is not enough to maintain personal balance and integrity within the ever-shifting but largely predetermined forces of the world and its history. What is necessary is to discern how those forces might be transformed for the universal common good and to act creatively toward that goal. That, in turn, means sharing, refining, applying, and promoting the vision in ever widening dialogues. It also requires efforts to understand ever more complex interpersonal, intergroup, economic, social, political, religious, and cultural situations and issues.

As Christians try to respond to their redemptive calling, there is always a risk of being so entrammeled in the complexities of these issues, situations, and social processes as to lose a steady focus on the goal that can never be known in concrete definition beforehand. There is also the opposite risk of seeing the goal as though it could quite simply be known in concrete definition, ignoring the complexities and denying inevitable ambiguity and ambivalence. The possible practical choices implied by both those risks have, in our times, and perhaps in all times, been the cause of rather bitter argument among deeply committed fellow Christians. This has particularly happened in relation to large political, economic, and international issues. It has occurred also in relation to the handing on of the faith to future generations and in relation to adaptations of life and worship in changing cultural contexts.

This book explores some dimensions of the personal challenges in the complexities of real-life contexts when values seem to be in conflict.

Chapter One

CONFORMITY AND CRITICAL DISSENT

As we emerge from childhood, we have heard many times how we are expected to behave, what are the proper courtesies to observe, what topics are not talked about with whom, how to relate to authorities, who are the people with whom we should not consort, how to present ourselves to be acceptable in society, what are the rules for many kinds of interaction. The general message is that society has established laws and customs, and we are expected to "fit in." Such messages come not only from the civil society, through family, school, neighborhood, sports and recreational activities, places of work, and so forth. Such messages about what are right behaviors and relationships, attitudes, speech, and ways of doing things also come very strongly from the church.

The persistence with which this message of conformity is inculcated is easy to understand. No society would be able to function without a large measure of predictability in the behavior and relationships of its members, all designed in patterns that make the interaction and common life possible without disruption. To make such predictability easier to achieve, common attitudes, beliefs, and expectations are inculcated, for the most part very effectively. The easiest society to run would, in fact, be one in which the members refrained entirely from critical and evaluative thinking about the values and expectations of their society. We have seen this in bold profile in modern times in the fiercely repressive measures used by totalitarian regimes to crush any yearnings among their peoples for the democratic freedoms these people could observe in other nations. We have seen denial of freedom of information through press and media, freedom of speech and assembly, freedom of religious practice and religious education, free elections of representative government, and much more. And, to a large extent, people have allowed these freedoms to be withheld from them out of constant fear, in exchange for an improved basic standard of living, or simply because it is easier to conform to expectations than to stand up and object.

It is characteristic of the modern age in Western industrial and postindustrial nations that we have come to recognize that such suppression of critical thought and expression is an evil. It is evil for two main reasons: it means that the great majority of people are not permitted to develop the adult maturity inherent in their nature and personhood, but it also means that so much power is concentrated in the hands of so few that the temptations to misuse it are great. Moreover, these temptations are frequently not recognized as such by those in power, and this is especially so where it is a case of the spiritual and moral power that goes with religious authority. We have seen this, for example, in its gross form in a number of Christian cult movements and in a number of militant Islamic extremist groups. We see it more subtly in the Catholic Church when

Roman curial officials forbid even the discussion of certain controversial issues.

This much has become very obvious in our time. What is less obvious is the extent to which demands for conformity and control of thought and expression are happening constantly and without any obvious violence in the situations in which we ourselves live. I am using the word conformity in this chapter to express the attitude that accepts many things as outside the realm in which personal critical thought and expression can or should operate. Basically, the word means "fitting into the prevailing shape of things." It is, therefore, in anyone's value system, in the first place a good thing. To become and to be a mature human person, it is certainly necessary to be guided in many things by the patterns of behavior that society has worked out, by expectations that are in place, by the recognized experts honored in the society, as well as by the laws and customs, by existing ethical and practical teaching, by those in charge of the common good of society, and by acknowledged thinkers on human issues. Anyone who would not learn from all of these or would not ordinarily follow them would be very foolish. To become and to be a mature believer, it is likewise necessary to be taught and guided by the religious traditions, the religious authorities of the church, and the teaching and example of recognized holy people.

However, what has become increasingly obvious in our times is that this apparently good attitude of conformity can be practiced with an unreflective exclusivity that makes it counter-productive in relation to its own end. From the good secularist's point of view, that end is simply to live a good human life, contributing to a good human society in prudence, justice, fortitude, and temperance. It is a matter of providing the best conditions for human life as inclusively as possible for all individuals and peoples. And most of the time, progress toward this is achieved by conformity to the prevailing expectations. It would not be helpful, for instance, to flout the traffic laws, although they are clearly arbitrary and could have been constructed differently. Yet there may be a time when, in contravention of the established laws, it is better to dash out and stop the traffic to prevent it hitting a fallen person or a disabled vehicle. Keeping appointments promptly and coming in time to community functions is reasonable behavior in response to reasonable expectations. Yet on occasion there may be overwhelming reasons for a delay that keeps everyone waiting. Ordinarily, there are reasonable expectations of repayment of debts, performance of the work for which one is paid, quiet and orderly behavior in public places, and such like, although some elements of each of these are arbitrary. But there are rare moments in which it is better not to conform to these expectations. And to recognize those rare moments when they occur, one must have a habit of critical reflection as well as a set of criteria by which to judge when nonconformity is required.

Because, for the most part, conforming to expectations without much critical reflection is a good thing and makes for a good society, it is not always easy to discern which common expectations should not be taken for granted but must be evaluated. For centuries after the European voyages of discovery, all types of devout Christians did not question the assumption that they could go into other continents to occupy and rule the lands of other peoples. They seem to have seen it as the natural progress of civilization. In the southern United States, for many years those who were apparently good people did not question all the assumptions and expectations that went with slavery. A Catholic moral theology manual of that time treated slavery only under the category of property rights. The author of that manual and those who used it in seminary teaching were apparently devoutly religious priests who saw no contradiction in this manual to the gospel of Jesus Christ. Even after slavery ended, many otherwise good Christians did not question the expectation that African American people went to the back of the bus or stood so that Euro Americans might ride in more comfort, or that African Americans had no access to the common drinking fountains, restaurants, or swimming pools. Many people conformed uncritically to these expectations even where they were not reinforced explicitly by law. Some people, however, did not conform uncritically. They distinguished between legitimate and illegitimate social expectations. They did this out of philosophical or out of religious grounds. In either case, critique and judgment of social expectations is exercised in relation to the end for which we believe the societal structures and expectations exist.

From a believer's perspective, the ultimate goal for which the life of individuals and societies is structured is the holiness, wholeness, and full communion with the transcendent God of individual persons and of all creation. But Christian believers also know that moving toward this is not the simple and direct route that this formulation suggests. The immediate and practical concern is liberation from the existing distorting effects of personal and communal sinfulness. An intermediate goal, therefore, is to create structures of society that set people free to see, judge, and act authentically and redemptively. Both the explicit and the more subtle structures of society are or should be geared to guiding people to act in harmony with the creator. While this is a positive and liberating goal, the road to it is often by restriction and restraint. Augustine of Hippo who wrote "Love and do as you will" also instructed his catechists to make sure that before converts heard that message, they should have become thoroughly familiar with the Ten Commandments. The laws of society have prohibitions against killing, stealing, and bearing false witness against others, and these are laws with heavy sanctions. Beyond the law, the expectations of society demand loyalty in marriages and other relationships, courtesy and fair dealing, consideration for the convenience of others, and so forth. These have more subtle sanctions, but the sanctions are there. Generally, in the day-to-day life of human societies, these work for good. From a believer's perspective, to follow the laws and societal expectations is usually the right thing to do as a matter of distinguishing right from wrong.

But there are exceptions, and to miss the exceptions can be disastrous. This is something that education and socialization, both in secular society and in the church, do not usually tell us. It is frequently in retrospect, and because of terrible consequences following on conformity, that the evil of conformity in certain matters appears. Some specific examples are worth reflection. A recurring example in human history is loyalty in time of war. At such time, the expectation generally agreed upon is "Love your own people and hate your enemies." The enemy is demonized or dehumanized to arouse popular support of the war. Often enough in history, Christians have believed that they were fighting for God's victory, and they have been able to believe this on both sides of the same conflict. The general expectations of their own societies have carried them along so that they have not even remembered the Gospel imperative, "Love your enemies." How strong such societal expectations can be is evident in the harsh treatment of conscientious objectors by other devout Christians, who implicitly hold loyalty to one's own side as superseding the command to love enemies. In doing this, they deny the right of the conscientious objector to critique the societal expectations in the light of the gospel.

To see and evaluate the expectations of society in the light of the end for which the Christian believer understands societal controls to exist is a far more strenuous spirituality than our common religious emphasis on conformity would suggest. It requires constant vigilance and reflection to see the issues inherent in daily life among the many circumstances, events, and relationships that are taken for granted in one's society. It also calls for considerable courage to act on one's own tested and well-reflected conclusions. Not only is there always the risk of being wrong, but such exercise of one's own conscience often finds itself up against much opposition and blame, even from fellow Christians. Again, some examples may make this clear, and we do not need to go as far back as the Crusades and the Spanish Inquisition.

One example from Europe is that of the Oberammergau passion plays. For many, many generations, the townsfolk of Oberammergau had put on a passion play every ten years to which people came from all over the world. It involved an immense amount of work for the whole town and was regarded as a work of great piety, an act of both worship and catechesis. Rooted as much in the history of Europe as in the gospel accounts, the unchanging script had bitterly anti-Semitic passages. When the townsfolk received a request to change these in accord with historical research into the trial and death of Jesus, and as a gesture of respect and fairness toward contemporary Jews, their first very firm response was a refusal. They saw the play not only as a whole but every detail of the text as a sacred trust, a communal Christian vocation of the town to which they were called to be true. The text of the play had taken on the authority of Scripture itself. Those involved could not see that there was anything wrong with vilifying the Jews in the play. It took long, patient, respectful intervention by outsiders to show the insiders what the problem was. Besides, even the outside intervention by Christians probably only came out of retrospective reflection on the experience of the terrible Nazi persecution of the Jews. And even in this context, it was difficult for the leaders to change what had the reverent adherence of the whole town.

Examples like this call for critical reflection on what false values and expectations may be hidden from our eyes in our own society in our own time. It should prompt respect for other people's conscience and discernment when they step out of line. It also calls for reflection on how one can achieve the balance of becoming appropriately critical while loyal to one's church and society. Beyond this, it raises the question of the kind of education and Christian formation required to bring believers to a maturity that allows them to be loyally critical of the institutions to which they belong. The Society of Friends, generally known as Quakers, has done this more successfully than most Christian denominations. Quakers have spoken up fearlessly in many situations where they had much to lose. Among the earliest generations, women preached publicly although they were ridiculed, arrested, flogged, and mistreated because they discerned that they were called to testify as believers on issues of the times. The pioneer Quaker conscientious objectors in Britain faced firing squads for refusing to fight in World War I, and died calmly, protesting their loyalty to the country but to God first. Against the general sense of the colonial Americans, early Quakers of Pennsylvania understood, and acted on the understanding, that the indigenous Americans were entitled to respect and friendship, not to ruthless conquest by superior weaponry.

These were not isolated cases of rare visionary individuals but rather common counter-cultural stances taken on Christian principles. They suggest, therefore, that there are elements of the religious formation of Quakers that tends to lead people to form and follow their own conscience with a certain blending of independent critical assessment with loyalty to institutions and traditions. Certainly Quakers are exhorted to obey, but it is first and foremost obedience to the voice of God, the Holy Spirit, heard within one's own informed consciousness. External authorities should support this but are not the ultimate criterion. In order to hear the voice of God, to tune in to the Holy Spirit, one needs to pray in silence with attention, cultivating the habit of silence to the point of being able truly to listen. And to do this, one also needs to cultivate simplicity of lifestyle and truth in relationships, as well as respect for the conscience and discernment of others. There are many imitable elements here. Those who live simply have less to lose. They tend to be more adaptable in their habits, their consumption, and their relationships, and therefore readier to take risks for conscience's sake. And those who are deeply rooted in silent personal prayer can have more confidence in their personal discernment.

Such examples as those of the outstanding Quakers raise the question whether not only society at large but also the church can be too insistent on conformity. If believers understand that conformity is always the spiritually safe option, the prophetic element of Christian faith is being suppressed. And that, in turn, means that the dynamic of the redemption is being obstructed. This is especially a risk in Catholic and high church contexts where much is expected of sacramental efficacy, with the danger that redemption is expected to come about through fidelity to sacramental worship without much emphasis on the need for radical change in the practical lives and relationships of individuals and societies. Too sharp a focus on remaining within the structures, following the observances, and staying out of trouble could work against the fostering of critical and prophetic exercise of conscience, whether in personal, professional, or public life. Unless the essentially prophetic, redemptive character of the Christian commitment is honored, taught, and emphasized, most Christians will settle quietly into the routine of established observances and never realize that a critical dimension of the faith is missing.

It is a common experience in human communities that in retrospect we appreciate and praise what at the time of the action was generally and authoritatively held to be blameworthy. One need but think of the leaders of the American Revolution, who were seen as traitors by many Americans at that time but in retrospect are seen as champions of liberty, justice, and truth. In another example, those who advocated and worked toward the liberation of slaves were first seen as making an attack on rights of property and on the good order and tranquility of society. In our own time, those who advocate and work toward gun control in the United States are considered by many as flouting constitutional rights and thereby attacking the public good. One wonders how this will be regarded in retrospect when Americans have had further experience of the exponential increase both in the incidences of violence and in the power of the weapons themselves. At the time of the Vietnam War, many American Catholics considered Catholic conscientious objectors as confused and arrogant on the grounds that "the" Catholic position was not pacifism but the Just War theory, and that the determination whether a particular war was just belonged to the government and not to the individual or even the church. Not only military recruiters but church representatives frequently gave these young men a hard time. Yet, even before the war was over, conscientious people of all persuasions had begun to look at that war very critically. And in the decades that followed, papal pronouncements became sharper and sharper about the evils of modern warfare and the need to ban war altogether as a means of resolving conflict and trying to right injustices. In retrospect, we begin to see those conscientious objectors as prophetic.

Perhaps the starkest example of this was the case of Franz Jaegerstaetter, an ordinary Austrian citizen but a great reader of the Bible, who refused to serve in Hitler's army after the Anschluss, the annexation of Austria by the Nazis. Not only was it the prevailing sense among fellow Austrians that there was no option but to go along with the draft, but Jaegerstaetter was assured, first by his pastor and later by his bishop, that as a Catholic he must certainly join Hitler's army because Hitler was in the struggle against communism. Jaegerstaetter steadfastly refused and was executed. In retrospect, we have no difficulty in seeing that his was a clear-eyed and courageous stance, not only in tune with the gospel but shrewd in discerning where the Nazi opposition to communism was really going. It behooves us as Christians both to imitate Jaegerstaetter's courage in our own discernments and to be open to the possibility that those we condemn for not conforming may be the true prophets of our time.

Chapter Two

OBEDIENCE AND DISCERNMENT

The sharpest confrontation of values occurs in situations in which personal discernment of the right path comes up against explicit law or the explicit command of authority. As most of us have been educated, we have been given to believe that in the contexts in which we live, a moral issue over an explicit law or command is very unlikely to arise. Yet this is a false estimate. The early twenty-first century has been marked by increasingly scandalous revelations of manipulation of evidence to justify wars of aggression, revelations of manipulative accounting and insider trading to grasp wealth fraudulently, of cover-ups of crime by professional and church people, of manipulation of elections, and much more. It is not only in other cultures and in countries that do not share our professed values that sharp conflicts can arise. In any country, any business, any profession there are contradictions between the professed values and the operative values and expectations. In such cases, officials at all levels of government, employers, shareholders, and employees of companies, individuals in any profession, quite frequently are given explicit commands to implement policies or perform actions that are outright immoral, are marginally dishonest, or do not offer the best stewardship or care of clients. Often the customary procedures are so well established that they are taken for granted as "the way things are," and the morally unwary are lulled into unquestioning obedience to commands.

Any education, and especially a religious education, that places too heavy an emphasis on the duty of obedience to rightful authority may well lead people to be blind to certain important distinctions. In the first place, not everyone who claims authority really has it before God. When a highjacker points a gun at an adult and says "Hands up, turn around and march" in an authoritative voice, the victim may conform because the attacker has power but will have no hesitation in escaping when the opportunity presents itself because the adult victim knows power does not constitute authority. However, when a kidnapper says in a firm tone of voice to a child, "Put your toys down, don't fuss, and come along with me," the child, who is used to all sorts of adults having authority and who is not in a position to distinguish, is likely to obey trustingly. That is why we have to defend children so diligently. There are certain parallels to this in the case of unsophisticated peasants in relation to landowners and employers, in the case of new immigrants who do not know the language in relation to those ready to exploit them, and in the case of minority groups who form a permanent underclass in relation to almost anyone with more education who acts in a way asserting authority. The vulnerability of these people rests on two factors. Everything in their lives has taught them to obey uncritically, which is a learned attitude, and nothing in their lives has equipped them with the intellectual skills to distinguish between power and authority, which is an educational deficit.

In successful dictatorships and military regimes, the majority of the people are kept in this state of ignorance and impotence, and trespass by authority on the personal lives and decisions of such people goes unnoticed. From time immemorial, the same policy has been a key factor in the training of armies and the conduct of military operations. It was this factor among others that caused the Christian communities of the first three centuries to conclude that Christians could not serve in the military. It is this factor that we recognize so clearly in retrospect in such cases as the My Lai incident of the Vietnam War, in the Abu Ghraib incident in the second Iraq war, and which increasingly we come to question in retrospect about the atom bombs dropped on Hiroshima and Nagasaki. The question about military (that is, unquestioning) obedience resounds around the world in relation to torture, in relation to the killing of civilians, whether intended or incidental, and eventually in relation to all killing and destruction, and therefore service in any war.

But we should not ignore the fact that it can happen also in religious contexts, and that this is not only in cults and strange sects, but in any church that asserts hierarchic authority with great emphasis. It was certainly a feature of the formation in religious congregations of women in the Catholic Church in recent centuries. The dictum that "the voice of the superior is the voice of God" was generally taken very literally, and access to information was often denied, even where that information was relevant to making moral judgments about a command. The mass exodus of women religious from their congregations after the Second

Vatican Council must certainly be seen in the context of this customary teaching of religious obedience when it was evaluated in the light of the Council's teaching of the responsibilities of the baptized.

What is critical here is not only that people under such dictatorships are deprived of basic human freedom to participate in shaping society and evaluating the issues that arise. Even more important is the truth that one cannot surrender one's responsibility before God for one's own judgments of conscience. Even those who have lawful authority do not have the authority to command immoral acts. This applies to all authority because all authority is ultimately subject to God. Whether in government, in the professions, in business, in the family, or in the church, no one has authority to demand lies to protect the organization, or a cover-up of misdoing to protect an individual, or actions that are financially dishonest, or injustices against individuals or groups. This is not universally acknowledged as is clear from scandals that have rocked major institutions, including the churches—financial and pedophilia cover-up scandals, to name only two. Many people in these situations, who should have spoken up, maintained silence in obedience to authority, and those who did speak up were in many cases discredited and disgraced. It is evident that the religious formation of some Christians had been such that unquestioning obedience seemed to exempt them from moral scrutiny of what they were commanded to do. It seems that, until the public revelations shocked people on a large scale, the disgrace earlier heaped on those who had spoken up only served to confirm to those who remained silent that this latter had been the right thing to do.

It is important, further, to acknowledge that even those who have lawful authority may not have as much authority as they claim or may not have it in all those matters in which they claim it. This is a distinction that the poor and uneducated are not able to make in relation to the police and other kinds of officials, thereby allowing for human rights abuses and various kinds of bullying and even extortion. Again, in the case of children this is a pervasive and inherent problem, especially with adult relatives, teachers, and clergy. The shocking incidence of pedophilia on the part of these three classes of people rests on the fact that children know these people really have authority and one ought to obey them, but, on the other hand, the children are not well equipped to distinguish clearly the actual range and scope of the authority these adults have. This increases, of course, the scandal on the part of those who take advantage, and one can readily identify with the words of Jesus about the millstone. It must be pointed out, in addition, that the more religious education stresses unquestioning obedience rather than personal conscience formation and critical assessment, the more vulnerable we make our children. They should, even from an early age, be respected when they ask "Why?" and should be allowed to debate issues about what is right or wrong and why this is so. "Because authority says so" is an answer that will not serve child or adult in the struggle for redemption in the real world.

The failure to make these distinctions about who truly has authority and in what matters they truly have authority arises not only among children and among uneducated and oppressed people. The most startling secular examples in modern history are those that came to light in the

Nuremberg trials of war criminals. There, the Nazi death camp operatives repeatedly explained to their judges that the duty of obedience to authority overrode any judgment of their own consciences. They did not distinguish between legitimate commands and immoral ones. Most of these death camp officials were Christians, many of them Catholics. Testimony was given about them that they were good husbands and fathers, responsible workers, and good people. They maintained the silence expected of them about the death camps and their gas chambers and went home to a good family life. They knew themselves to be good people because they obeyed orders punctiliously—all orders, without distinction. Given that this is an extreme case, it nevertheless raises an important question. What had happened in the Christian formation of these people that allowed them so easily to equate their obedience to the Nazi regime in the running of the death camps with obeying the will of God?

This is an extreme case and now seems remote from the issues we face in our own lives, but are there not many lesser instances in which teaching, preaching, and catechesis have been stressing the obligation to obey in a way that seems to brush aside the responsibility of individual conscience to weigh conflicting values? The major scandals of the early twenty-first century mentioned above certainly suggest that this is so. This is even more prevalent when the question is not one of outright immorality, but one of prudential judgments of what is best. In most cases, those who want to keep their jobs, maintain their position in an institutional structure, or advance in an organization will find it expedient to do as they are told, whether or not it is the best for those whom the organization is supposed to serve. Hence, organizations are able to skimp on the services they are supposed to provide, as has become evident with for-profit health organizations, for instance, where the investment returns may be controlling the medical decisions. Similarly, manufacturers are able to pay unconscionably low wages by transferring factories to poor and dependent countries or by employing undocumented immigrants who cannot establish a right in the civil law to protest.

On a somewhat analogous basis, banks are able to charge outrageous interest loans to their poorest borrowers because these have poor credit ratings that are made generally accessible, guaranteeing that they will not be able to borrow at a better rate elsewhere and will sink into permanent crushing indebtedness. Employers are able to hire unskilled workers, even in the United States, at a minimum-wage level at which the workers cannot support themselves, not to mention their children, at a basic level of human dignity and family privacy. One of the most critical issues in our times is the manufacture and sale of armaments, ranging from major instruments of war to the ready availability of handguns for street violence. People are employed in making and distributing them. Many have investments in their production, as for instance in the way company and collective annuity funds are invested. All of us are responsible for what is happening in our economy, from which we profit.

These conditions and many more situations of injustice are possible because almost all of those involved are quietly doing what they are told to do. They are not doing anything obviously evil, but they are also not taking responsibility for the policies they are implementing. Cumulatively, what is being done in these enterprises achieves oppressive and unjust conditions and provides the means for a great deal of violence in the world. If Christian believers were not satisfied with obeying what they were told to do in their jobs but were scrutinizing their own responsibilities and activities by the criterion of the Reign of God and its demands for justice, compassion, inclusive community, and peace, they might speak up and perhaps lose their jobs or forfeit promotion. If enough of them did it, they might have an impact. This is not, of course, an easy decision from any point of view. Not only do people have to weigh their responsibilities to their families when contemplating truly prophetic actions with consequent risks, they also have to calculate where and how they might best have an influence that will work toward what is better and when and where they would be wasting what possibilities of influence they might have.

All of this suggests a spirituality that requires far more reflection and courage than does an uncritical and therefore unquestioning obedience to all authority. That such personal responsibility may be demanded by the profession of Christian discipleship raises logically the delicate question of how this applies to the balance of obedience and discernment in relation to the church itself, and for Catholics especially, in relation to the hierarchic church with its Canon Law and its various specific teachings.

It is, of course, well known that the Catholic peoples geographically and culturally closest to Rome have not traditionally had the same attitude to Canon Law and to specific church teachings as that generally taken for granted in the English-speaking world—a fact that has often puzzled the latter. In the secular sphere, we English speakers are accustomed to a minimalist attitude to legislation. We usually make laws only when there is, or is very likely to be, a problem. We distinguish among three categories: first, the most fundamental laws that make up the constitution of the country, whether written, as in the United States, or understood in the tradition of the courts, as in Britain; second, those other laws that are important and serviceable but are more easily changed to fit need; and third, regulations such as traffic laws. They have various degrees of importance to us, ranging from those that are close to the essence of the country's values to those that are purely arbitrary arrangements for convenience. However, we tend to assume that while they are in place, we need to obey them all literally or work through legitimate channels to get them changed.

The Canon Law of the church is not like that. Based on Roman Law, and more particularly on the very inclusive Code of Justinian, Canon Law takes a maximalist approach to legislation, attempting to give a tidy and inclusive picture of the whole life and organization of the Christian community in all its component parts. Clearly, this means that as a worldwide code it needs local adaptation. That is what the Mediterranean Catholic peoples have understood and have done informally by their discriminating patterns of observance. If assent to the law does not preclude adaptations and exceptions, this calls for local and personal responsibility in discernment of how the law applies. The Mediterranean Catholics apply this to explicit teachings of church authority outside of Canon Law also. This can, of course, be abused in self-serving and not quite honest adaptations, but in itself this attitude is not one of rejection of church teaching but one of adult adherence—an appropriately adult obedience.

In our time, as the changes of the Second Vatican Council have slowly (and not always smoothly) come into play, Catholics of the northern European and English-language cultures have come to take on something of that stance in relation to church teachings. This may often have been a fairly thoughtless drift into gradually ignoring church teachings altogether. Clearly, a truly adult obedience is not the same thing as doing what one "feels like," or what is easiest, though there are, of course, people who do this last. Nor is it the same thing as ignoring the teaching in favor of using one's own judgment, though there are also people who do that. A mature adult obedience is an attitude and a praxis that is more complex and a great deal more demanding than its various substitutes and impostures. In the first place, it presupposes a thorough knowledge of the tradition, a deep and affectionate reverence for church authority, well-established habits of personal prayer and meditation, and an intellectual and practical humility that is always open to listening attentively to contrary opinion.

As none of us can ever be quite sure we entirely match the description in the last sentence, great discretion is suggested in the exercise of adult obedience. Among other considerations essential in the transition from adolescence to adulthood is the ability to see accurately where the knowledge drawn from one's own experience needs the complement of the cumulative wisdom from the experience and reflection of others. This is true in all aspects of life. Yet as difficult, not to say impossible, as this is, we are clearly called to this level of human and Christian maturity, and one aspect of its exercise is to respect the consciences and decisions of others, especially those who differ.

A common experience at this time, especially in the United States, is that truly committed Catholics see the legitimate scope for personal discernment in different areas of human activity. Some who see every detail of the current sexual teaching of the church as clear, essentially permanent, and absolutely beyond discussion will nevertheless judge in good faith that the church's explicit teaching may be disputed on capital punishment, a whole range of social justice issues connected with the critique of the capitalist systems in existence, the justifiability of particular wars, the evils of weapon production and stockpiling, the interpretation of personal property rights, and of responsibility for those left out by law and economy. On the other hand, there are Catholics, also in good faith, who see the church's teaching on these social issues as so clearly and directly the expression of the task of the redemption in the world that they are beyond debate, while better knowledge of the history of the church's sexual teachings shows that they have developed and changed as conditions of life and knowledge of biology, sociology, and psychology changed and continue to do so. Respect for one another's consciences and discernment might make all of us wiser in discipleship of Jesus Christ.

Chapter Three

HUMILITY AND THE USES OF POWER

Most of the events of the last century enumerated in the Introduction and first two chapters of this book were matters of the use or misuse of power and the success or failure of others to challenge those who misused power, often on a grand scale. The argument in the first two chapters was that heavy emphasis in church teaching on compliance and obedience to authority needs a counter-force for balance. For Christian education, catechesis, and preaching to be true to the message of the redemption and the call of the Reign of God, they need an equal emphasis on the, prophetic aspect of the Christian vocation. Those chapters, therefore, were addressed to those governed, those under authority, those who do not seem to have any power over public affairs, whether economic, political, social, professional, or cultural. That is how most of us see ourselves most of the time, as though we did not have power over others or over public affairs.

Yet, in fact, all of us do have power or access to power far more than we usually admit. To the extent that we deny to ourselves that we have power, we fail to advert to how we are using it. We may be using it officiously, self-servingly, ambitiously, or unjustly, even oppressively. But far more likely, we are using it like the buried talent of the parable by withdrawal and nonengagement. Why else would it be possible that so much power should become progressively concentrated into so few hands where it is arrogantly used? This burial of the one talent may be a matter of laziness, or of failure to realize what is happening, or of timidity and fear of taking risks and responsibilities. But for Christians, there is another issue also. There is an apparent conflict of values between the persistent teaching of humility and the sort of assertiveness that is required in wielding power.

It is often evident in worldly and in church affairs that the safest people to be entrusted with power and authority are those who have no hunger for it, but these people tend to escape it while the power-hungry are always at hand when a vacuum occurs. Moreover, so expert are human beings at deceiving themselves that power-hungry people often see themselves as simply eager to serve. Perhaps the most difficult aspect of this is that those in possession of power, especially those who have a strong monopoly on power in a given situation, seldom recognize their own motives in clinging to their exclusive control. They will see clinging to power as their obligation to maintain the good order of the society or community. How powerful this is can be seen by the disparate voices and forces, many of them religious spokespersons, who blame and condemn movements for economic liberation of the poor, even when these take the peaceful shape of building cooperatives of production and marketing. There seems to be a perennial dilemma about the acquisition, possession, and use of power.

When Christian voices blame the poor for wanting to take control of their own lives, the people of occupied lands for wanting independent self-rule, women for wanting access to leadership and decision-making roles in civil society and church, minority groups for wanting equal participation, workers for wanting mass bargaining power, and so forth, it is often with the assumption that the present distribution of power is the will of God, and that people should accept it as such. Hence, any attempt at community organization of powerless groups raises two kinds of issues about humility and the uses of power. It raises a question about those who take the initiative to organize, thereby claiming leadership and inevitably also power for themselves. It raises a second kind of question in relation to those whom they organize because it means arousing in these people what is essentially discontent with their present situation—in other words, a hunger for more power.

The first thing to be said about this in a Christian context is that the teaching on humility calls for careful reflection. The Gospel testimony about humility is essentially narrative and consists of the following. Mary's song, the *magnificat*, praises God who lifts up the lowly but brings down princes. The young Jesus submits to the authority of his parents, and the adult Jesus submits to the baptism of John with the prophetic implications it has of assuming the calling of Israel to surrender itself wholly to God. Entering on his public ministry, Jesus declares in the synagogue of Nazareth that he has come as the liberator of the Isaian prophecy, someone whose mission is to challenge and reverse many things. In his public ministry he mixes alike with rich and poor, respectable and disreputable, the learned and the peasants, the devout and public sinners, treating everyone with respect and taking all equally seriously. He clearly expects his disciples to do the same. In this context he tells many parables with a reversal theme: in God's eyes, things look very different from the way they appear in human society.

In this context also, he exhorts his followers not to try to be important by worldly estimates, to think of their mission in terms of service rather than domination, to be willing to take the last place, to have no more pretensions than small children, to be plain in speech and generous in action. Finally, in his arrest, trial, and passion, Jesus is shown challenging those in whose power he is. He tells those who come to arrest him to let his followers go free. He challenges the servant who strikes him in court with the illegality of the action—a cruelty often inflicted on bound and defenseless prisoners, then and now. In speaking to Pilate, he points out the perilous situation in which Pilate himself is placed. Confronted with Herod, he challenges him with his silence.

If we look to the person of Jesus as a model of humility and to his teaching for clues to the humility appropriate to a Christian, we do not find in them simple acceptance of whatever is in place in human society. What seems rather to emerge from the Gospels is a way of seeing relationships as they really are before God and acting on this quietly and courageously. And, indeed, as Christian theology and philosophy have reflected on what true humility is, they have proposed that it is the recognition and acknowledgment of one's true relationship with God, with other people, and with all creation. It is based on truth, but this is not the factual truth of where and how one is placed in human society. Thus, the truth on which the humility of a slave should be based is not in slavery but in the slave's human personhood and dignity before God. The truth on which the humility of a crushed peasantry or a permanent underclass should be based is not in the facts of their wretchedness and oppression, but in their calling as human persons to live exercising their full humanity. Hence, to call oppressed people to discovery and appropriation of their full humanity is not in itself arrogant and does not call them to arrogance, though it may, of course, be done arrogantly by those whose motives and self-knowledge are not well ordered. It is also true, as all who work on consciousness raising and community organizing know, that in calling people to their true dignity and freedom, one takes the risk that they will overassert themselves, turn to violence, try to turn the tables by oppressing others, and so forth. But none of the risks means that the project of liberation from oppression is in itself arrogant in the eyes of God.

To be truly humble before God is necessarily to get oneself in trouble with those committed to existing arrangements of human society that are not in tune with the Reign of God. There is a conflict of values here, but this is not the difficult one because it is clear to the person who engages in liberating and community building activities among the oppressed or marginalized. The difficult conflict of values is the one within the mind and heart of the liberator or community organizer. It is the tension between realizing the importance of humility in a Christian life and the realization that the situation calls for self-assertion and the deliberate acquisition of power to act and to lead people in action. Community organizing depends on accumulating the power of numbers. It depends on the kind of leadership that excites and incites people to keep coming and keep committed to the common goal. There is a certain amount of showmanship in it. There is a discovery of one's own power to lead, one's influence over others, one's power to get them to do things, to move masses, to confront the established power, forcing it to shift and accommodate. There is a subtle, and perhaps not so subtle, temptation to enjoy and pursue the use of power for its own sake and to be seduced by it into what is no longer a purely liberating action for others. Power, of course, gives a person importance, status, privileges. Power implies success, achievement, and certain liberties not granted to others. In other words, power is horribly seductive, drawing its possessor to the very antithesis of Christian values.

If transformations of social structures are important, and if such transformations depend on the use of power, then there must in the divine dispensation be the possibility of wielding power without being spiritually and psychologically destroyed by it. But traditional Christian spiritual theology has little to say in praise of acquiring and wielding power, whereas it has much to say about the importance of humility and of making modest claims in the world. This imbalance can leave a thoughtful and deeply committed Christian with a puzzling dilemma as to how to act. Congregations of vowed religious have one kind of solution to this with the vow of obedience. Traditionally (though not always in contemporary practice where there may be more personal choice), members of congregations go where they are sent and do the work that is assigned to them whether it is important in a worldly sense or not, whether they are in positions of command and control or not. They do what they are sent to do because they have made the prior commitment of vowed obedience. This may sound very straightforward and easy, though vowed religious seldom seem to find it so. But the more basic concern is with the Christian life when people are free to make their own decisions about the important initiatives in their lives.

The first step in thinking this through seems to be to admit that there is a real tension between values here and a real risk of missing the balance. That risk is not a matter of imagination, undue fearfulness, or personal shyness. It is real risk, and it has to be taken into account. A second step might be a closer look at what power is. When Black Power was seen as an overwhelming threat to American society in the Civil Rights Movement, Martin Luther King pointed out that this apparently threatening word did not in itself imply violence or oppression but was simply "the ability to get things done." Indeed, power could be viewed on a long continuum, stretching all the way from love power to kill power. Along most of that continuum, power as the ability to get things done includes the empowerment of others, and this is the goal and intent of consciousness raising and community organization.

But what sets out to be love power and empowerment of others can very easily deteriorate into manipulation that actually disempowers. And this certainly happens in crowd incitement. It can be extreme, as happened in the mass hysteria of Hitler's and Mussolini's crowds, for instance. Or it can be mild and subtle, as happens with a good deal of community organization when it is not based on building true consensus but on sweeping people off their feet in the excitement of mass action. It is particularly pernicious when those carried along in this way are being incited to an action that puts them or others at great risk. It is noteworthy that Mahatma Gandhi always insisted that he did not want excited, swept-away crowds for his nonviolent protests. He

31

wanted people who had trained themselves by a long asceticism of nonviolence, reflection, simplicity of lifestyle, manual labor, and consequent modest economic independence. He wanted people who acted out of their own deeply held convictions, not out of dependence on his convictions. For this he was willing to wait, meditate, and fast.

The third step in thinking through the tension of values involved in the conscientious and responsible use of power has to do with one's own self-knowledge and self-discipline. How does one come to an effective focus and scrutiny of one's own use of power? It seems there must be external and internal checks. As to the external checks, we all need people who are not so prejudiced in our favor that their judgment is untrustworthy. We need these people to speak the truth to us as they see it, clearly and without glossing over any of it. Dictators and rabble-rousers have always surrounded themselves with yes-men. That is why they have been able to misuse power in unconscionable ways. The problem in trying to meet this requirement of external checks is that those who engage in action for social transformation are sustained in it by consorting with others who have the same goals. They discuss and strategize together, seldom hearing divergent opinions.

It is surely this, for example, that has led to unfortunate and counter-productive actions so frequently in the peace movement. Speaking always with one another, these very dedicated and selfless people have not been able to see what was evident to neutral observers about attacks on missiles and missile sites. Actions that seemed to peace activists to speak powerfully of the evils of war, in fact, appeared to others as in themselves violent and provocative of counter-violence. In these cases, the peace activists acted from selfless idealism that could, however, turn into bitterness and failure to listen to well-meaning critics. Conversation that is too exclusively with like-minded activists tends to dispense with the external checks on the way power is being used. A similar critique can be made of the less productive initiatives of Black Power in the United States—initiatives that provoked brutal repression by the forces of law and public opinion. Needless to say, such repression in turn tends to embitter the activists and corrupt their motivation with unbridled anger and revenge. In these cases, the external checks were missing because other voices in the black community, some with great wisdom, were not given a hearing.

Though difficult, it is clearly important to have external checks of the use of power. They need to be concerned with the rightness of the goals, the congruence of the actions with the goals, and the wisdom of these actions in their actual present context. To have external critics who can do this is already more than is usually available. However, even if it were available it would not be enough. In the use of power there also need to be internal checks of well-developed clarity of purpose, self-knowledge, self-discipline, and a habit of constant evaluation. Without any one of these components, power is guaranteed to corrupt. Together they constitute the practice of humility in the use of power. Perhaps that humility begins with the realization that one is corruptible, no matter how clear the initial goals and motivations. From that beginning, humility is practiced by using the resources of the tradition to develop the above four components.

Christian tradition has great resources, in the first place, to develop clarity of purpose. Meditation on both Scripture and church doctrine brings into focus the over-arching goal of welcoming the Reign of God in all creation. Persistent prayer and meditation evaluates intermediate goals in relation to that final goal. The context of a living, worshipping church community should be a strong support in this, but that does not always happen. Those who are drawn to prophetic, socially transforming initiatives often find devout fellow worshippers uncritical of social injustices and therefore unsupportive. Often, the long-term church tradition offers better role models and support than the church community present here and now. It is, however, necessary to listen respectfully and attentively to the community of believers that is present to make sure one has really heard them before deciding it is necessary to differ from them. Moreover, clarity of purpose is not something achieved once and for all, but rather something that needs to be renewed constantly.

Foundational in the necessary internal checks for the use of power is certainly self-knowledge. Not only Christians and other religious people value self-knowledge. The ancient pagan Greek philosophers set great store by it. Self-knowledge is easier to praise and value than to attain. The resources that Christian tradition offers are basically a well thought-out moral teaching, a habit of examination of conscience in relation to that moral teaching and in a context of prayer, a sacramental practice of repentance and reconciliation, spiritual direction, and spiritual conversation and friendship. History shows that by some of these means even absolute monarchs like the Emperor Theodosius can be brought to a radical self-critique concerning the use of power. Those who set out to defend and empower the underprivileged are ordinarily both personally better disposed and socially better placed to gain self-knowledge than is the well-established despot. This does not apply in the same way to those who for good reasons enter the conventional political process, standing for election or seeking appointments. They enter a process where success depends on playing the game by the rules. The conflict between the tacit rules of the political process and the believer's criteria for the proper use of power may be sharp. The Carter administration in the United States was some indication of how sharp that conflict can be for a conscientious and seriously religious person. Yet no matter how sharp a conflict of values is involved, it cannot be a reason for committed Christians and other conscientious people to refrain from political engagement or positions of power in society, a matter to which the two following chapters of this volume return.

Along with self-knowledge goes self-discipline. Essentially, this means internalizing not only commandments and rules but the principles and motivation on which these are founded. The resources that Christian tradition offers include not only teachings in morality and spirituality but also sacramental and other structures of community support, such as the celebration of the liturgical year, the observance of Sunday, and regular participation in the sacramental life and outreach activities of the local church community. However, self-discipline in everything, including the use of power, is essentially an individual challenge and responsibility. The ancient Greeks honored the challenge mainly under the categories of fortitude and temperance. There is, on the one hand, the need to face and take on many things that are arduous, tedious, risk-filled, painful, or otherwise repugnant. All of these are certainly involved in the proper use of power. Then there is, on the other hand, the need to control and moderate engagement in what is pleasurable, easy, entertaining, and flattering. All of these are seductive in the possession and use of power. One must know one's own attractions and repugnances in order to maintain the balance.

It will be evident from the above that it would be impossible to maintain clarity of purpose, self-knowledge, and self-discipline without a constant process of evaluation. It may be this last in particular that is lacking when the use of power acquired for the best reasons and with the best motives begins to corrupt. Especially in the contemporary postmodern, postindustrialist world of the economically overdeveloped countries of the West, power corrupts very quickly. The speed of change, the multiplicity of distractions and preoccupations, the anonymity of many of the decision makers, the reduction of people to statistics, and the remoteness of the impact of decisions in many cases all contribute to a muddying of the issues in which exigent evaluation of the use and impact of power can fail to happen. Some aspects of what is at stake are considered in the following chapters.

Chapter Four

LOYALTY AND THE
DEMANDS OF TRUTH

One of the values we are taught most insistently in both secular and church contexts is the need for loyalty. It begins with loyalty to one's family. We are taught that not only should we support our families in contributing to a good, inclusive, cooperative, and courteous home life but that family affairs are kept in the family. One does not speak critically of parents or spouse outside the family, one does not "wash the dirty linen in public" or discredit the family in any way. This is obviously good and basic to human community life. There are usually some disagreements and quarrels in a family, but they are also ordinarily best settled without drawing outsiders into them. This contributes to the security and sense of comfortable at-homeness that people should be able to enjoy in their families. And this applies not only to individual households but to the extended family, which offers a network of supportive relationships. As families are the basic units of human society, this is for the welfare not only of the individuals but also of the society as a whole.

What we have learned, however, through crime statistics, social services, and wider knowledge of psychology is that family loyalty cannot safely be proposed as an absolute. It must be kept in a prudent balance with the demands of truth. The mother who warns her children not to tell anyone about sexual abuse by father or uncle is not so much loyal to the latter as disloyal to the children because the truth must be known so that the abuse can be stopped and the children supported in dealing with the traumatic memories and in recovering trust of adults. Similarly, there comes a time when spouse, children, or other relatives must turn to persons outside the family for help in dealing with an alcoholic or addicted member. Yet, because loyalty has often been preached so much more insistently than the demands of truth, many people find this very difficult to do and continue to feel guilty when they have done so. The reason for feeling guilty is, of course, that there is a real conflict of values and that there is no way of meeting both demands in a kind of textbook purity and simplicity. It is necessary to balance the values and act without the guarantee that the action is the very best that could have been done, and without guarantee that it will turn out well and not cause further suffering.

What is true of the family has parallels in the professions. From time to time, scandals hit the news headlines of concealment by medical doctors, police officers, lawyers, research scientists, social workers, accounting and engineering firms of something that has gone wrong from human error or carelessness or of something that was dishonest or unlawful. The socialization of people in the professions includes a powerfully persuasive sense that above all they must be loyal to their peers in the field and close ranks against criticism or attack. This is certainly good to the extent that they should not sabotage one another's work, reputation, or clientele. But there is a tendency to place that loyalty even above fiduciary responsibilities to patients, clients, or the public. It is not strange that this tendency should exist. There is mutual protection in these peer group loyalties. Members have a strong incentive to protect any member at risk in the expectation of getting the same protection when needed. The reason that this provokes outrage when discovered is, of course, that outsiders can sustain harm from it. It is an important case in which the demand for truth is more important than the commitment to loyalty. However, it is clear that whistle-blowers always suffer for stepping out of line in the name of truth and honesty. They perform a prophetic function, and prophets, as Jesus himself said, are not appreciated until long dead. Moreover, the whistle-blower, no matter how tactful and gentle in approach, threatens not only the individual whose misdeeds are exposed but also the system of mutual protection and therefore is seen as dangerous by all.

These issues are raised to a higher level when matters of government are concerned, when public policy is based on concealment of pertinent facts. It is not accidental that the term "spin doctors" has entered our vocabulary. The assumption behind the term is the normalcy of the practice of so selecting, arranging, disguising, concealing, or even distorting the facts that they support a predetermined policy or decision, usually for the benefit of the rich and powerful. This is evidently seen as loyalty to one's party or candidate. But the consequence is that democracy is mocked because the people are kept confused or uninformed, and in practice harm is done, often to the poor and powerless or to the heritage of future generations and frequently enough to the global ecology and the well-being of other nations. Even from a secularist ethical perspective, these are situations in which the demands of truth are stronger than those of loyalty. Security seems to be in the latter because the fate of whistle-blowers is well known. They are fired from their employment, ostracized, and persecuted, if not actually assassinated. Finding the right balance between loyalty and truth calls for great courage, not only because testifying to the unwelcome truth is generally not applauded until well after one's death but because there is often lingering internal doubt about whether one has done the right thing.

It is especially in foreign policy and international affairs that such issues become very tense. In retrospect, we know that the saturation bombing of the residential city of Dresden in World War II was unnecessary and strategically not significant. Looking back, we have access to the documented testimonies that the dropping of atom bombs on Hiroshima and Nagasaki happened when the surrender of the Japanese in the same war had already been signaled and this information had been suppressed. In retrospect, we know that it was on the basis of fabricated testimony that the Gulf of Tonkin Resolution launched a long and terrible war against Vietnam that no one could win and that caused suffering and death to an incalculable extent. Civil wars around the world have been launched on misinformation and the magnifying of old grievances for operative motivations that had little to do with the professed ones. In recent history, we now know that the professed grounds on which the second war against Iraq was launched were based on untrue allegations. Over this issue, at least one whistle-blower in Britain went to his death, demonstrating again both the inherent risk of what he did and the courage required to speak the truth against claims of patriotic loyalty. In principle, most would admit that wars should not be launched on the basis of lies or even on the basis of uncertain information. Yet again and again what moved most of those concerned was a sense of loyalty that made them unwilling to criticize the actions of their own government in a context of actual or imminent war.

This troubling history of general connivance in the suppression or blurring of truth in the cause of loyalty, with only occasional heroic figures standing out and paying the penalty, is a challenge to all of us about the ways we balance our loyalties with the demands of the truth. The stakes are not always as high as in the examples above. Yet the question arises whether these examples were only possible in the context of a more general ethos of giving loyalties precedence over truth. Ordinarily we expect religious figures to give some guidance and personal examples in this, and certainly some have done so. On the world stage, one thinks of Mahatma Gandhi and the Dalai Lama, not to mention many of their followers. Among Catholic leaders, bishops like Helder Camara and Oscar Romero, and outstanding priests like the murdered Jesuits of El Salvador come to mind. But in the internal affairs of the church, the actual course of events is more worrying.

In the United States, and just as spectacularly elsewhere, the clergy pedophilia crisis and its long and confusing aftermath brought to light the extent to which the hierarchic church operates on some of the same assumptions as secular governments about the overriding importance of loyalty to the institution and of protection of its public image. The concealment of crime from the representatives of the law of the land and the unwillingness of some dioceses to allow a subsequent audit of both the criminal activity and the finances involved shocked many. Even more so were many thoughtful Catholics concerned when statements came out of the Roman curia reinterpreting the crisis as one of sensationalism and prejudice in the press rather than admitting that the abuse itself, the failure to take measures to stop it, and the concealment of what was going on were terrible evils. While the sins of the press are many, the sensationalism did not cause the problem; it only made it more salacious when it had already happened.

On the specific issues of the clergy pedophilia incidents and the inaction and cover-up by some dioceses, action was taken and safeguards gradually put in place, though not without a fierce and prolonged struggle. The question that remains to haunt reflective and attentive Catholics, both lay and clerical, concerns the institutional culture out of which this crisis arose. And at the heart of that question about the culture is the tension between loyalty to the institution and the demands of the truth. This is a question that goes far beyond the pedophilia crisis. It concerns the pastoral responsibilities of the bishops in the local churches. It concerns communications within the entire institutional structure on a global scale. And it concerns the bases on which decisions concerning the life and worship of Catholic communities around the world are made. If loyalty to the accustomed ways and assumptions of the Roman curia takes precedence over the facts of the actual situation in the world and the local bishops' own assessment of the pastoral needs of their dioceses, there is a serious denial of truth involved. And this has consequences for the life and mission of the local churches that may be disastrous in the scandal both to those inside the church and those outside.

It seems to have been this concern that led Pope John XXIII to call the Second Vatican Council. He expressed the desire to "open the windows" of the church to the world. He spoke of *aggiornamento*, of bringing the church into the reality of the present. The Council itself spoke of the collegiality of the bishops, the active vocation of the baptized, the concern of the church with the transformation of the world, the importance of religious freedom, positive evaluation of the role of the other religions, and so forth. It was all directed to knowing and acknowledging the truth about the world and the peoples living in it. Many Catholics who had experienced their Catholicism as something rather detached from the affairs of the world, an enclosure that kept believers safe and separated from the world, had a sense of waking up, coming into a freer atmosphere where they could act as adults and trust their own experience. Some did, of course, overassert their freedom and the value of their experience, but the breakthrough to a fuller and more personal Christian life was on the whole authentic. What has happened in the church in the decades since the Council has frequently seemed like a struggle between lively local churches and regressive moves from the curia to reimpose pre–Vatican II patterns of church life, ignoring or denying the reality of the contemporary world, forcing the living languages of the liturgy into Latinized artificiality draining its meaning, and reestablishing the sense of an ontological chasm between clergy and laity that leaves the former isolated and the latter passive.

What has happened here bears some analogies with the ways in which the tension between loyalties and the demands of truth were tragically resolved in the secular examples cited above. In both cases there is the problem of shaping policy and behavior to match the preferred self-image and public image of the institutional body in disregard of the available evidence of the truth of the situation. The church no longer launches wars as it did in the time of the Crusades nor even encourages them as some prelates did rather openly in the anticommunist era. In fact, John XXIII, Paul VI, and John Paul II have constantly campaigned against the justification for any war in our time of mass destruction. But the consequences of denying the facts of pastoral needs and contexts can be drastic in its crippling of the ongoing redemption of the world through its transformation for peace, community, and inclusivity. There is a justified concern that what appeared so glaringly in the pedophilia crisis is the tip of an iceberg of denial of the reality of whatever does not fit the preconceived image projected from the Roman curia onto the local churches. It requires great wisdom, courage, and restraint to act faithfully and constructively in this context.

The human project of integrating personal authenticity and truth with the difficult task of being a community and loyal to one another in overlapping patterns of increasing complexity is not easy. It is full of inherent tension. We do not come to the project with a clean slate and a fresh start. We benefit from the ways our cultures and traditions have already built the bridges and the communications. But we are hampered by the untruths, distortions, and infidelities that have also shaped the world we inherit. Yet as Christian believers we see ourselves graced with revelation and located within the process of the redemption. This does not exempt us from efforts at transformation. It empowers us in those efforts to see truth and act on it.

Chapter Five

ABSOLUTES AND COMPROMISES

Among the more difficult tensions of a conscientious life is that between absolute demands of morality and unavoidable compromises of living in society. Both morality and religious beliefs are often presented in absolutes, especially in the biblically derived faiths. The claims and demands of God are absolute because there is but one God and no other beside that God; therefore obedience to God has no legitimate compromises. All this is true, but complications set in as soon as we ask how we are to know the will and command of God. Many authorities claim to be divinely appointed representatives and interpreters. Moreover, the options and possibilities life offers us turn out not to fit into neat categories and distinctly black and white patterns. One is sometimes left to discern which is the lesser of two evils because they cannot both be avoided. Many choices and decisions have to be made without clear knowledge of all the relevant information. In most issues in public life, and in the common life of large groups, the best that can be done is to bring the possible a little closer to the desirable.

Any steps in that direction are largely a gamble—a wager as to how much cooperation will be forthcoming. Asking for too much will mean failure of the whole initiative, whereas asking for too little will alienate the most promising collaborators and bring the project to a standstill.

In the biblically based traditions, it was established at the outset that the nonnegotiable baseline of the morality God demands is expressed in the Ten Commandments. Much else must be extrapolated about further implications for a good life and a good society, but these ten commands are the absolutely nonnegotiable baseline. Practically all adherents of the biblically based traditions will grant this. Yet among the seven commands of the second tablet, "You shall not kill" is certainly the most basic, in spite of which many of the most rigid adherents to the letter of the law totally exempt themselves from this commandment in the context of war. In Christian tradition we have built an elaborate collection of "Just War" theories. There are arguments about the circumstances that justify going to war and arguments about what circumstances justify what kinds of killing and destruction within a war. True believers have further exempted themselves in having those found guilty of grave crimes executed, even in circumstances where the system has been shown faulty in executing innocent persons among the guilty. Most Christians in the United States support immigration laws that force certain categories of people back from the borders to certain death by starvation or assassination. Most support policies and tax structures that guarantee high rates of infant mortality among marginalized populations from malnutrition and lack of medical care.

Most of these actions and tacit assent to them do, in fact, sink very far below the acknowledged nonnegotiable baseline of the morality we know God commands. They constitute a moral compromise of momentous proportions, even if people are so used to them that they do not see their incongruity. In the Catholic community, this moral compromise of such vast proportions has become almost invisible because of the one-issue focus on abortion. The deaths of enemy civilians as well as combatants, deaths of those condemned by criminal or immigration laws, and deaths from deprivation of means of livelihood have tended to be obscured in Catholic consciousness by the focus on abortion. Respect for life must, of course, include the unborn, our own as well as those whose mothers are in populations at high risk from bombing, poverty, mass killing of peasant populations, and other man-made risks. But surely it must also include those already born and struggling in the world, especially the most powerless among these.

When one factors in the preliminary observations above about the inevitable compromises in a human life, and especially in public life, as well as the above observation about the extent to which we have compromised the non-negotiable commandment against killing, it may be easier to understand the dilemma about public responsibility of believers in relation to the legality of abortion in a pluralistic country. It is necessary to bring the possible as close as can be done to the desirable. This is a prudential decision at each point for each legislator, each executive, and each judge. A purist or absolutist position would eventually require all faithful Catholics to withdraw from public life and also from the health professions as services are progressively concentrated under large corporate bodies subject to legal controls. It brings the Catholic community up against the tension between the absolute command not to kill and the

realization that it is not possible to function in society without compromise. It is the same as the dilemma in relation to
the country's wars, the existence of the death penalty, and
policies that guarantee a high infant mortality rate among the
poor and marginalized. Those who support this latter list are
already deeply compromised in relation to the commandment
not to kill, and they cannot salve their consciences by focus-
ing on the one issue of legalized abortion. Strangely, though
the last three popes have spoken and written repeatedly and
emphatically against the justification of war under contemporary conditions, many Catholic intellectuals continue to
consider this a matter of opinion while reducing respect for
life to questions of abortion and euthanasia.

It is not only in relation to the fifth commandment
that the tension of the absolute command and the practical
compromise arises. It happens in relation to the commandment, "Thou shalt not steal," though in less obvious ways.
The biblical context of the commandment was very different from today's economy. The formerly enslaved and land-
less people had been brought into a land of their own that
was then parceled out by tribes and families. Laws were put
in place that guaranteed the periodic return to the family
that originally owned it of land that was lost or given away
or heavily mortgaged. Land played the role that land and
capital jointly play today. It was the only means of gaining
a livelihood. The commandment against stealing was mod-
erated not only by this arrangement of the return of the
rightful share of land, but also by laws that allowed
strangers, widows, and orphans, for example, to glean from
other people's fields after the harvesters went by. Moreover,
landowners were to instruct the harvesters to leave the cor-
ners of the fields for these gleaners. The combined effect of

such arrangements was supposed to be that everyone got a share of the fruits of the land. The early Christian community tried to put similar inclusive arrangements in place with the understanding that those who had a surplus of possessions would not consider it their own but make it available for the needy of the community. In the fourth century, Ambrose of Milan had no hesitation in writing that Christians who had wealth that they did not need had stolen it from the poor. He obviously did not mean that they had gone to the houses of the poor to take things away but that the economy amounted to theft if it created so large a gap between rich and poor that the latter were desperately needy in the presence of great wealth.

By these standards, most of us in the United States are badly compromised over the seventh commandment also. We live on land that was taken from the original inhabitants by violence, leaving them such scarce resources that as ethnic groups they have almost died out, and most of the survivors live in destitution and hopelessness. We benefit from prosperity built in part by uncompensated slave labor, which is equivalent to the theft of wages. We eat disproportionately cheap food and wear disproportionately cheap clothing because many of those who produce these now are living in inhuman conditions on wages inadequate to support human life in dignity. It is in this context that we need to look at some of the apparent absolutes connected with the claimed rights of private property. For some time, papal encyclicals and other papal teachings have pointed out that the right of private property is not an absolute allowing indefinite accumulation in the hands of the few while many live in extreme poverty and while progressively more people of the world are reduced to poverty. What church teaching proposes as an absolute is that workers have a right to their share of the product of their work and that this must at least be a living wage for themselves and their dependents.

Those of us who are not employers are nevertheless involved in this through the investment of our retirement funds, through our purchasing habits, and through the companies for which we work and the companies that provide us with various services. For conscientious people, this is a burden in our times that constantly calls for resolving a tension between absolute moral demands and the practical need for compromises in order to live and function in our society at all. It is not possible for any individual to track down the sources of all one's consumer goods and services to find out whether contractors and subcontractors are paying honest wages and maintaining decent working conditions. Neither can the individual voter find time to examine all budget and other legislative proposals, although these are critical in determining whether all have just access to goods and opportunities. Fortunately, there are many voluntary organizations that have and use the resources to trace and analyze these dispositions, and one can follow their guidance. Yet no matter how consciously we try to live, we are forced by the complexity of the issues to make many compromises.

This leads to the question whether there are then no absolutes. One might certainly suggest, "You shall not commit adultery" and "You shall not bear false witness against your neighbor," as it is difficult to think of any circumstances in which it would be morally better to do either of these things. However, more broadly Christian tradition does maintain that there are absolutes. They are principles against which to measure possible actions, though it may not be possible to define them concretely in specific actions in a way that is beyond dispute. Certainly, "Love your neighbor as yourself" is an absolute for Christians, while its precise embodiment in varying circumstances cannot be spelled out beyond dispute. In other words, there will still be a broad range of prudential decisions and discernments required in choosing the best policy to welcome and accommodate refugees, or to help the destitute, or to set up a welfare system. The more conscientious people are, the more likely it is that they will have considerable concerns about whether they are too ready to compromise on the commandment of love of neighbor.

In this matter of absolutes and compromises, the beginning of wisdom is to recognize the problem that there is no such thing as a perfect and demonstrably blameless solution. The next step is to be continuously about the business of forming one's conscience by study of Scripture and tradition on the one hand and on the other by becoming progressively better informed about the facts of one's society. Neither is expendable. To know the facts is not enough for evaluation. We tend to take the state of affairs in our own society for granted and not to see what is wrong in God's eyes. On the other hand, to acquire a great sensitivity of conscience and compassion from the study and practice of one's faith does not of itself bring a correct understanding of the economic, political, and cultural dynamics of one's society. A further step in addressing the challenge is certainly to think issues through with other committed believers and to consult knowledgeable persons, whether or not they are believers. After all this, it is usually not possible to act on significant social issues alone; therefore, a key challenge of compromise is to find ways of action that a sufficiently equipped group can agree upon.

When all of this is done, most conscientious people will have a sense of disappointment that there has been too much compromise.

Nowhere is this more constrictive than in political activity in the public realm. When serious accusations are made by church leaders and certain lay proponents against legislators, judges, or others about compromise positions, the accusers generally evince a lack of understanding of these restraints. A legislator can seldom get a piece of legislation through as drafted by this one person. To get it into law the individual has to work on building an alliance and a consensus and that is done by endless painstaking compromises. A single item in the end product of a piece of legislation cannot be used to judge whether a particular senator or congressman is a faithful Catholic, one who can, for instance, be invited to give a college commencement address. A judge usually has some discretion but does have to administer the law of the land, even in those aspects with which that judge does not agree. An administrator of a publicly funded program has to follow the guidelines and regulations for the program, even where some may be against that administrator's personal religious convictions. In these cases, the choice between absolute adherence or compromise is really only whether the issue is of such overriding importance that it is better to resign from the office altogether or whether more good can be done by remaining and using the influence of the position to move the doable a little closer to the desirable. In the case of the legislator, the only choice is probably between abstaining from voting and from initiating or endorsing proposed legislation (which guarantees loss of the next election) or, on the other hand, making the best compromises that have a chance of success.

More usually, when the accusations of infidelity are made against Catholics in public positions by some of their fellow Catholics, it is also because the latter are applying a one-issue scrutiny to a multi-issue task. Occasionally, such scrutiny comes from Catholic social activists who may be concerned only about immigration or welfare or peace issues. But more often it comes from those who focus their entire concern on abortion. This is, of course, a critical issue, but it is by no means the only issue even in terms of respect for life. Nor can one assume that a personal position against abortion logically or in conscience requires a legislator to work to implement this as national policy. It may, for instance, be evident that there is so little support for it that it would be a frivolous law with no hope of being observed. It may be evident that the result would be that abortions would continue to be performed but without the legal and medical restraints otherwise in place. It may be clear that change must happen but that it must be brought about in the culture first to such an extent that a law can be effective. There has been a tendency in this one issue of abortion to allow no tension or scope for prudential judgment between the demand of the absolute value of life and the need for some compromise in public legislation in order to achieve any progress at all. On the other hand, there has been broad tolerance of compromises in congressional voting on war powers and other life issues. This is not consistent.

In the last analysis, personal resolution of the tension between the absolute demand and the practical possibility in any situation or task is a lonely matter. The individual has to wrestle with it and come to a prudential decision. There are sure to be people who think any particular decision wrong and out of step with religious faith in the particular tradition. It would, however, be a better world if they would refrain from accusations of immorality and infidelity when someone else's prudential decision does not coincide with their own.

Chapter Six

LAW AND JUSTICE

The tension between law and justice cuts across most of the foregoing. Governments, police, courts of justice, and most commercial enterprises function as though law and justice were the same reality. But if they were the same, there would be no basis for the critique of law and legal systems. Nevertheless, public life is often carried on as though they were the same. For instance, an "ethics" inquiry in the U.S. Congress is generally an investigation to find out whether some public figure or organization has profited by contravening the laws and regulations that pertain to the transactions at issue. Spontaneously, however, neutral observers often realize that justice is not being done, even when they are not able to put into words exactly their reasons for holding this conviction and when there is no transgression of the letter of the law.

In fact, throughout history absolute monarchs and dictatorial regimes have always wanted to establish explicitly and dogmatically this equation of the existing law of their regime with justice so that there could be no appeal of any sort against the regime and its laws and customs. Throughout history, such regimes have given us martyrs, heroic figures who spoke out or practiced some form of civil disobedience on grounds of conscience, supported either by reason alone or more often by some religious tradition. In the Western religious tradition, Hebrews first and Christians later were persecuted for just this cause. They proclaimed that there is only one God to whom all are answerable. The immediate corollary to this is that the ruler of the land and the law of the land do not hold absolute authority. There is a higher court of appeal beyond the law of the land. On the basis of this, one not only may but should sometimes oppose the ruler and the law.

In lands of Christian heritage, most of us have been educated to assume that occasions calling on us to resist and act against the law will be very rare. We assume it is very unlikely to occur even once in our individual lives. Yet one of the earliest proclamations about the one God of biblical faith is that God's ways are not our own respectably established human ways. God's ways are far above our human ways and always challenging the latter. In other words, the justice of God can never be equated with any human code of law, even that of the most Christian country imaginable, even the church's Code of Canon Law. All codes are subject to critique by the justice of God. One may not, in the ultimate analysis, surrender one's own conscience to any authority, any law, any code. Such authorities should, of course, be respected. There is a presumption in their favor as one begins to reflect on any issue. In most cases, there will be no need to reject that presumption.

Yet the history of the world's affairs makes it very clear how easily most human beings can miss the issues where the general presumption in favor of the law should have been questioned in the particular case. Authority should indeed be respected, but it is only one factor in the forming of one's conscience on any matter. Other factors are experience and the innate ability to distinguish between right and wrong. Cumulative human wisdom from many sources, including one's own religious tradition, offers a range of resources for forming one's conscience. Learning to see human affairs as God sees them is a lifetime effort to use all these sources wisely. Moreover, it is a lifetime effort to grow beyond prejudice, partiality, ignorance, and self-interest, not to mention anger and revenge, laziness, and ir-responsibility. Among less-than-perfect people in a less-than-perfect society, human individuals and communities never know the justice of God concretely, comprehensively, and definitively.

This is the heart of the challenge for any conscientious person. Justice, as noted above, is one of the four cardinal or hinge virtues. It is very important, not only in its impact on society but in its shaping of the character of the individual. To live a good, integrated, balanced, and focused life, one must act justly in all one's relationships and activities. But there are no blueprints for this. There are some ground rules like the Ten Commandments, the moral substance of which is generally accepted by people of all traditions, including secularists and theoretical atheists. However, as noted in chapter 5, such basic ground rules call for a lot of extrapolation. The laws we have are some efforts at extrapolation from the ground rules. Besides the law of the land, these include rules and regulations of various professional and occupational organizations and the laws and rules of churches and other religious bodies. All of these laws are man-made, subject to the limitations of those who made them—the limits of their experience, their prejudices, and their tendencies to take the patterns of their own society as "natural" or God-given and therefore unquestionable.

A conscientious person sees two consequences of this. The first is easy: it is not enough to obey the laws; justice may require going beyond the law. The second is difficult: justice may require going against the law. As to the first, there are many good examples in everyday life. Conscientious employers in the contemporary United States do, in fact, realize that justice requires them to pay more than the legislated minimum wage because the minimum wage will not sustain an employee in decent living conditions. Conscientious professional people will go beyond the guarantees that the professional regulations provide, putting the client's interests ahead of their own convenience. The choice in such examples is easy, not perhaps in terms of the sacrifices they might involve but in terms of thinking through what is the right thing to do. It is from that point of view that deciding to go against the law is more difficult.

There are many examples of people who went against a law from conscientious motives. In retrospect, it is often clear whether it was the right or the wrong thing to do. When faced with the choice beforehand, it is not always easy to know this. There is also a much larger number of examples of problem situations in which people should have acted against the law for reasons of conscience but did not do so. At the time the action was called for, these people either did not have the courage to act against the law or they did not understand that justice required it. Both opposing and not opposing law raise the question of how one is supposed to know the right thing to do. This is not only a question of acting justly. Justice is closely related to prudence, and prudence is a matter of using the right means to an appropriate end. The means need to be proportionate to the end and adapted to achieving the end. Hence, for instance, those anti-abortion protesters who fatally shot physicians of abortion clinics no doubt saw a legal system that allows abortion as unjust and therefore saw themselves as entitled to go against the law by killing in defense of the lives of the defenseless unborn. But the actions were inappropriate to the end because killing to protest killing adds further injustice, gives the wrong message, and fails to achieve its purpose of preventing further abortions. Even had they burned the clinics down, the activities would move to another building. The action truly appropriate to the end of preventing abortions is the tedious, unheroic, unspectacular long-term process of trying to change public opinion, the culture of sexual behavior, and the legislation of the country.

The shooting of the abortionists was an extreme case. Some cases of peace activism in the latter half of the twentieth century were more complex and less obvious. In various actions at various times, they contested the legality of war and weapons production by contravening security and property laws. But the laws that they broke were not laws that were in contention. A conscientious judgment that all war or a particular war is unjust leads logically to refusal of military service, lobbying of government and legislature, public demonstrations, and other actions directly and effectively aimed at trying to stop war or armaments production. A conscientious judgment that the arms race is unjust would logically lead to the boycotting of anything that contributes to it, even if such actions are against the law of the land. But trespassing and damaging property are breaches of laws that are patently just and necessary. Such actions are inappropriate to the end and also in themselves unjust. Therefore, they were also bound to be counter-productive. Ordinary reasonable and conscientious people would not be persuaded by such lawbreaking.

A more subtle case is that of the American student crushed to death because she interposed her body between the Israeli tanks and the homes of the Palestinian civilians that the tanks had come to destroy. She was protesting a real injustice and she was risking only herself. Her death made a powerful statement. Until the last moment, she probably did not think the tanks would really keep going and mow her down. Her action was aimed immediately at the defense of the families living in those houses and, beyond that, at the injustice of Israeli law in the long-occupied Palestinian territories. Yet one might still legitimately ask whether the means were appropriate to the end. The question is not easy to answer. She had the precedent of the nonviolent revolution in the Philippines when tanks with their machine guns mounted were stopped by unarmed bodies of priests, religious sisters and brothers, lay leaders and peasants. In that case, however, there had been a long preparation, the uprising had the blessing of the Catholic Church in a predominantly Catholic country, a huge number of supporters had been gathered, and it could be assumed that the sympathies of the lower ranks of the military were with the protesters. The all-time classic precedent of Mahatma Gandhi's self-rule campaign also opposed armed force with the nonviolence of unarmed people. But again there had been a long and rigorous preparation, a gathering of massive numbers of supporters trained in nonviolence, and the strength of the indigenous religious tradition. The American student seems to have acted spontaneously and alone. She was certainly a martyr for justice, less certainly an appropriately prudent one.

Yet had the Philippine march to oppose the tanks in the streets not been successful, we might well be judging in retrospect that it was neither just nor prudent for the leaders to expose their followers to such danger. At the time, they discerned the rights and wrongs of the situation and the possibilities of success as best they could. They calculated the probability of success as sufficient to justify the risks, but they could not possibly know for certain what the outcome would be. Similarly, in each march and each action, Gandhi and his confidants had to calculate risks without knowing beforehand with any certainty what the outcomes would be. Even today there are some who look back thoughtfully at that heroic movement to liberate a people and then ask whether anyone had the right to lead others into such slaughter and injury. (Note, however, that this is a question that must also be asked, along with so many others, about the legitimacy of war.)

What should one conclude from such examples? In the first place, prudence and justice go together: the means must be both appropriate and proportionate to the ends; one should not commit an unjust action to protest an injustice; and one should have reasonable chances of success when undertaking an action involving high risk, especially when the risk is to others. Second, there are usually several prudential decisions involved in which there is no black and white answer before engaging in the action. Third, like the law, the individual group that acts against the law is subject to human limitations. Even after they have gathered the fullest possible information, have prayed, have consulted, and have reflected in a careful and unhurried way, they may still be wrong. That risk always remains. It is perhaps this re-alization as much as anything else that keeps many good people from acting, especially if their personal and religious formation has given them no confidence in their own judg-ment and has perhaps even undermined their self-confidence in making moral judgments. Such formation leads people to assume that they are always morally as well as practically safer by not acting against the law, even when there seem to be serious questions.

This perspective on what is morally safer usually shifts in retrospect, at least when the action was successful or the inaction resulted in catastrophe. Most thoughtful people would probably say that the American Revolution, the American Civil War, the French Revolution, the fall of the Soviet empire, and the Third World independence move-ments of the twentieth century, all beginning with illegal ac-tions, made changes that were morally right though the means were open to question. Almost everyone today would say that those who disobeyed laws that kept slavery in place in the United States acted justly in helping slaves to escape even though this was against the law and inflicted economic harm on slave owners. This position is based on the judg-ment that slavery is an intrinsically unjust relationship and that basic human dignity takes precedence over property rights. History records, however, that conscientious people of the time of these events were sharply divided.

On the other side of history there are examples of in-action in the face of unjust laws. The Nazi era in Germany produced a progressive series of laws against employment of Jews in the professions and the arts, for the internment and execution of retarded people and gypsies, later for intern-ment of Jews and Polish intellectuals, not to mention many other repressive measures. It is often supposed that nothing could have stopped the catastrophic consequences of Hitler's actions, but he acquired power in stages and took repressive actions progressively. Mahatma Gandhi, on the basis of his own experience in South Africa and India, and after studying the course of events by which Hitler attained power and managed to keep and increase it, maintained that nonviolent resistance from the early stages could have averted the Second World War and the other horrors that took place. Evidently, most people during the Nazi era thought it safer to mind their own business, hoping the threat would pass without effort on their own part. And they thought this until it was too late.

To make any judgments about justice that transcend the law, one must have criteria for justice. One has to appeal to some understanding of what are right relationships among people. Modern declarations about human rights have drawn largely on the principles of the Enlightenment and the French Revolution, which place heavy emphasis on reason and reciprocity. Justice according to these principles means basically as much freedom for everyone as is consistent with the freedom of the others, with equality of opportunity, and fraternity, which means inclusion among the people that count, the people that are seen as the subject of history. Yet without drawing on the diminishing capital of the West's Christian history, the political structures, legal systems, and economies of most Western countries leave little freedom for large sections of the population because economic power rules everything, from party politics to differential restrictions on immigration, from the shape of education to access to housing and employment. Certainly, there is no equality of opportunity in the overwhelming discrepancies of wealth and of the power that wealth confers. And there is no fraternity in the way our economic, political, and legal systems progressively marginalize the poor.

It seems to be very difficult for many good people, Christians among them, to recognize that the operative values in our social systems are not the proclaimed national values. There has, for instance, been little protest or action when grossly underpaid cashiers and salespersons are daily arrested, tried, and visited with very disproportionate penalties for ridiculously small incidences of petty theft. Nor is there general recognition of injustice when families with both parents working full time and working extra jobs cannot find modest affordable housing. Voters and lobbyists and responsible citizens are confronted with a contrast between what the law guarantees in practice and what justice would require even by Enlightenment standards. When seen in the light of the doctrines of creation, sin, and redemption, and the equal dignity of all persons before God, the demands of justice become a great deal more exigent.

For believers, the tension between law and justice is most difficult to resolve in those issues that concern church law. Catholics especially have tended in recent centuries to regard church law as coming directly from God. This would equate law and justice so that there could be no further questions about matters of law. Sometimes this has even caused Catholics to put ritual obligations like attendance at Sunday Eucharist before very serious human claims as though any conflict had already been settled by the very existence of the ritual obligation. But the ritual obligations are man-made laws and so is the entire Code of Canon Law. The Code itself only dates from 1917, and in its present form was reshaped with much debate and reissued in 1983.

Particular edicts and prescriptions have changed very much in the course of time to accommodate changing circumstances. This was often because earlier versions were no longer appropriate and had, in fact, simply not been generally observed over long periods of time.

For most lay Catholics, conflicts with Canon Law do not arise very often except in relation to marriage. The refusal of the church to recognize remarriage after a divorce can leave some people with serious moral questions. There may already be basic human claims of justice in a second relationship. There may be considerations of the needs of children that are in conflict with requirements of Canon Law. In practice, many people do spontaneously what justice or the well-being of the family seems to require. But they do it with an uneasy conscience because their education has led them to think of church law as simply the same as the will of God. With this equation, they cannot even dare to think that a claim of justice could be stronger than the claim of Canon Law in God's eyes in this particular case. Many people feel that their choices have cut them off from the church, and they drop out of their parish community, losing the support that this community might well have continued to give them. Even more sadly, they may think that their choices have cut them off from God. In discussions of what it means to be a faithful Catholic, there is often an undiscriminating confusion of faith, morality, and Canon Law in which this last dominates.

Yet Jesus himself declared that the Sabbath exists for the people, not the reverse. It is clear that in the context of this gospel saying, Sabbath represented the entire ritual code. Similarly, in the story of the Good Samaritan, Jesus has the Priest and Levite turning away, which was necessary to maintain their ritual purity if, as it seems in the story, they were on their way to Temple service in their official capacity. The implication of the story is that the dire need of the wounded and abandoned man should have taken precedence over ritual obligation. In this and other Gospel stories, Jesus exhibits an order of values in which common sense and a right view of love of God and neighbor are the key elements in discerning what is just and right to do in particular circumstances.

The other issue that comes up constantly for many lay Catholics is not a matter of the ritual code but a moral position that has come to be regarded as law because of the way it has been asserted and because of the sacramental implications that it has. This is the question of contraception. Some Catholics regard the prohibition as simply the will of God, allowing for no discussion or question. In response, either they observe the prohibition or they consider themselves out of the church and probably in a state of grave sin. Other Catholics, knowing something of the history of the issue, have formed their conscience by looking at all aspects of the question in the light of the tradition and the discernments of conscientious people. They then act accordingly, either using or not using contraception, and remain active church members in good conscience.

In the late sixties of the twentieth century, however, a number of priests in the Diocese of Washington, DC, and elsewhere, concluded that there was a more urgent question of justice for them as priests. They took time to inform themselves about the long-term history of the issue, and about the intense debate over it in the papal post-Conciliar commission appointed to work out an answer. Then they declared jointly and publicly that, in justice to the faithful for whom they were ordained, they could not advise people in the sacrament of reconciliation that contraception was mortally sinful. Having spoken publicly, they were, of course, disciplined in various ways by church authority. This does not show that their decision was wrong. In the course of history many people have been disciplined by the Catholic Church and later been shown to have been prophetic in words and actions. People who break the law expect to incur the penalties of the law, but they may still be making the right choice. The reason that the choice to disobey a law is a difficult choice is precisely that it incurs the penalties of the law. It will also incur the unhesitating condemnation of those for whom the law is absolute, black and white in its clarity, and equated with the justice of God. Yet the disobedience may have been a correct discernment of the justice of the case in the eyes of God.

Chapter Seven

PATRIOTISM AND DISCIPLESHIP

Patriotism is one of the most serious obligations taught to almost everyone. It is taught with such solemnity and with such unanimity that it is not surprising to find many people who consider it absolute, taking precedence over all other values and obligations. It is one example of the general principle of loyalty discussed in chapter 4, but it is unique in the sweeping mass sentiment that it commands and in the universal reinforcement that it finds in the national context in which most people lead their entire lives. Patriotism has strong affective content that is consistently cultivated. It is cultivated through the honor and ceremony connected with the national flag, through maps that tend to show the nation's land as central on the earth, and through histories that exalt all that the nation has done and that put its actions in the best possible light. It is further promoted through festivals that celebrate the professed values and claimed accomplishments of the nation and keep the stories alive and through constant proclamations that its culture and its way of life are the best.

The claim that this is the right way for human beings to live is made both explicitly and implicitly. Moreover, people rightly become aware that their country, through its government and organization, has a great deal of control over them and also offers them many needed services. It issues forms of identification such as Social Security numbers that certify a variety of entitlements that belong to citizenship. It issues passports and visas and offers protection both at home and abroad to those recognized. Nothing is more important for a person's security in the sociopolitical world than to be a citizen, or recognized as a lawful inhabitant, of the country and therefore entitled to its protection. The nation supplies a complex network of public services that make physical and social life possible. In return, it demands an all-embracing loyalty that shapes the sense of identity, of belonging, and of social obligation.

Nevertheless, the claims of patriotism are not absolute, and whenever in history they have been treated as absolute, it has become a disaster. By common sense, we should know that patriotism cannot in reality be an absolute value because there would be as many absolutes as there are sovereign nations and the result could only be global chaos and a general holocaust. Beyond common sense, people of faith know that the only absolute is God and that all else is subject to God. The claims of one's country are necessarily subject to scrutiny by what we can know of the law and will of God. Expressed theoretically, this seems obvious. In practice, it is often not so. We commonly hear a very deceptive rhetoric. There is a great difference between two ways of invoking the name of God in political discourse. On the one hand, there is the rhetoric that claims God as the nation's champion and invokes the name of God as the sanction or endorsement of national policy in fact decided on self-interest. On the other hand, there is rhetoric that we almost never hear from those in power. If it is used at all, that will be from an oppositional voice. This is the plea to submit public policy to scrutiny by God's law, or by true justice among nations, or by consideration first for the poor and the excluded. The world has seen a great deal of the first type, the "spin" that subordinates God to the national interest as perceived by those in power. In the United States, where popular piety has remained strong, this kind of political rhetoric has become so bold that the phenomenon has been recognized and analyzed by sociologists. They have named it the Civil Religion.

The most noticeable characteristic of the Civil Religion is that it sees its own country as singularly favored and chosen by God to show the other countries of the world the right way to live and to organize their societies. If anything approaching such a claim appears to be made by a Muslim country and nation, Americans react with passion against such an evil, imperialist, and lawless mindset. In the days of the Soviet Empire, there was a similar perception and rejection of communism (though as an atheist tradition, communism did not invoke God but a kind of principle of intrinsic inevitability that could be hurried along a little for everyone's benefit). The old colonial regimes died because of a general rejection of the European sense of mission to "civilize" the world.

Yet when the United States, currently the wealthiest country with the most kill-power, proclaims the same kind of rhetoric, it is difficult for those within the society to see the likeness. It is difficult for them to realize that to the rest of the world, these kinds of claims are threatening and evil, whether they come from a European colonizer, Hitler's Nazi party, pre–World War II Japan, a communist state, a Muslim organization, or the United States.

What is common is the claim to be singularly favored and chosen to "save" the rest of the world by putting the other countries straight and under "appropriate" rule. From a believer's point of view, the Civil Religion, wherever it occurs, is idolatry because it usurps the prerogatives of God. To clothe this usurpation in the language of biblical and Christian piety does not change the reality. It puts a smoke screen in front of it, which tends to deceive the unwary. The immediate consequences of usurping the prerogatives of God is that the affairs of other parts of the world have meaning only insofar as they affect the chosen and favored country. We can see that so well in the above-named examples from the past. We can see it in what happened to the populations of countries colonized by England and Spain, for instance. We can see it in the dehumanization of the non-Aryan peoples by Hitler's regime, the fate of the Koreans under Japan, the East European and Central Asian peoples under Soviet rule, and so forth. But we see it also in the fate of Amerindians and captive West Africans in the United States, the disasters visited upon the people of Vietnam, Afghanistan, and Iraq, and of Cuba, Chile, El Salvador, and Colombia by various types of interventions to "save" them.

Another characteristic of the Civil Religion is to merge patriotism with religious piety to the point at which they become indistinguishable from each other while, in fact, for practical decisions patriotism has subsumed religious piety. There are many reasons for which two sets of American Christians are particularly vulnerable to this. The first set includes the Presbyterian and Reform Churches because they essentially built the early structures and traditions of the United States with the idea of making it a godly Christian nation. The Reform tradition, like the Catholic, is really committed to the Christian faith as having strong sociopolitical implications. The Enlightenment doctrine of separation of church and state sits quite awkwardly within the society that the Pilgrims hoped to shape. The original purpose of the separation doctrine was, of course, to prevent possibilities of religious persecution and discrimination—a purpose not so well attained in the history of the Irish and Italian immigration. But the outcome of the blending of Pilgrim intent with Enlightenment guarantee has unfortunately been the Civil Religion. Religious values are indeed invoked, but without the restraint and critique of authoritative church voices when the rhetoric is misappropriated and turned upside down.

Catholics are also vulnerable to the rhetoric that subtly subsumes religious loyalties under patriotic ones. Catholic civic consciousness in the United States is still deeply influenced by the immigrant experience of being suspect and often excluded in the economy, the culture, and the polity. Catholics have been very anxious to prove that they are loyal Americans "in spite of" being Catholic. They have been conscious of needing to demonstrate that the pope is not scheming to subvert the country by enticing away the loyalties of Catholic Americans. They have also been anxious to show that being Catholic does not equate with being stupid, uneducated, culturally backward, or naive. Many Catholics who are not recent immigrants still see themselves as a disadvantaged minority although, in fact, they are now the largest single religious denomination in the country and are relatively wealthy and relatively well represented in the corridors of power. With this background, it is easy to see that Catholics might have a strong, if unacknowledged, desire to find patriotism and religious faith in unquestionable harmony. Some can remember the days when Catholic schools and even churches displayed the national and papal flags side by side, like a visual assurance that there would be no conflict.

A third characteristic of the patriotism that expresses itself in the Civil Religion is that every war and every intervention in the affairs of other peoples becomes a holy war or a sacred saving mission. The problem inherent in holy wars is that they are perceived as abrogating some of the ordinary moral rules because of the sacredness of the cause. Incidents of torture are whitewashed with the appropriate "spin." Wars of naked aggression are justified because of the sacredness of the cause, such as the need to contain communism, to ensure or introduce democracy (by force), to prevent the development of weapons of mass destruction (except in one's own country and among its firm allies), to end cruel and violent regimes not friendly to one's own country (by warfare, which is inevitably itself cruel and violent). There is a similar problem with other types of intervention that purport to be fulfilling a sacred trust. The embargo intended to force Cuba to become the kind of democracy advocated by the United States has achieved only the further impoverishment of a country where many people are quite desperately poor. Military support to Colombia seems only to have increased armed conflict there and greatly increased the suffering of peasants and kidnapped people.

During the times that such wars and interventions have happened, many protesting voices have spoken, truly representing the religious traditions. This has included the persistent voices of several popes, who have argued both against the initiation of particular wars and against modern warfare in general as a means to solve any of the world's problems. They have been joined by representatives of other churches and other religious bodies. They have argued that there are no means to contain the violence once begun, that the feuding logic leads each war to beget another, that the main victims are children, the poor, and those who have least at stake. They have argued that diplomatic channels are greatly enhanced in our times and that they have a much better chance of attaining the declared objectives of these wars. They have pointed out that there are extensive grievances on both sides of every conflict and the sheer weight of military might will not put the grievances to rest or set matters right. Unfortunately, the rhetoric of the Civil Religion is very adept at drowning out these authentic religious voices or deflecting them with pious exhortations to participate in the crusade on God's side.

One of the consequences of the idolatrous claims on the part of sovereign nation-states is that such claims undermine all attempts to fashion and maintain international law and international administrative, legislative, and judicial bodies. The fact that, however awkwardly, these bodies are speaking for the common good of the nations on a global basis means that they are a move toward world peace and collaboration. That move is effectively thwarted by the refusal of the militarily strongest power to be guided by the decisions of the United Nations, or to submit its own military actions to the International Court, or even to pay dues promptly—all refusals made as a means of forcing compliance with partisan demands of one country. In the end, such refusal to collaborate and subordinate perceived national interest to the global common good is simply using the threat of economic and military power to dominate other nations and force compliance to the national interest of the strongest. It acts on the maxim that might is right. The rhetoric used, however, does not express the matter thus. It claims it has a better understanding of what is good for the others than they have themselves, or it impugns their motives in disagreeing with itself.

It is not only in questions of war and military interventions that a believer may find a considerable conflict of values between the demands of patriotism and those of discipleship. These conflicts certainly come up in relation to the treatment of undocumented aliens in the country. While it is true that, for reasons of public health and social and political stability, there have to be immigration laws and procedures, there are some critical issues. Two of these are the subtle and not so subtle uses of race and wealth in setting the differential categories for immigration. Another is the tacit unofficial tolerance of illegal immigrants employed in onerous and underpaid jobs with no rights or bargaining power while at the same time penalizing and deporting those who are caught in a sweeping operation from time to time. There is no doubt that the immigration laws are geared to keeping the country prosperous by keeping the poor of the world out and crowded into less fertile and less mineral-rich lands. From a believer's point of view, strangers, like widows and orphans, are entitled to special consideration.

It is a generally accepted idea of patriotism as we know it that the increasing wealth of one's own country takes precedence over economic conditions abroad, even when one's own country steadily profits at the expense of the poor nations that are progressively impoverished by their economic relations with this country. This can happen through the tax structure, through trade agreements, through moving manufacture from country to country in search of the cheapest labor, and through the raw force of bargaining power to set the relative values of what is produced abroad and what is produced at home. Ordinary people are involved in this as consumers, as subscribers to retirement funds, as voters with the power of lobbying, as members of political parties, as members of churches politically active on behalf of the poor, and as potential participants in various types of action and pressure groups. In all of these activities there are choices to make. Often they are made without much reflection, for personal convenience or preference. More informed people know that they are making choices that cumulatively lean toward perceived national or class self-interest or that cumulatively lean toward what is more just, more promoting of peace, more likely to give opportunities to the excluded.

Although individuals cannot be expert and knowledgeable in all fields of human commerce that have a bearing on the choices, there are church and public interest groups that do put the knowledge and expertise together and analyze the issues. Not all analysts and public interest groups look at the questions from the perspective that a committed believer should take. Some analyses place perceived national interest first and see this as the only reasonable criterion. Apart from the question of seeing the partisan interest of one's own nation as the ultimate criterion, which is idolatrous, there is another question. The national interest is often equated with the accumulation of wealth and power, no matter how access to these is distributed among the citizens. In the United States, political rhetoric often identifies wealth and power with God's blessing on the land. It takes no account of the fact that even in the twentieth century, large numbers of hard-working farm families were driven off the land into destitution by the unequal competition with huge accumulations of wealth in private hands. It takes no account of the fact that this unequal competition has also further impoverished the farmers of other continents who cannot compete. It is difficult to see God looking on this to bless it.

Many American Catholics are surprised to learn that recent popes, and especially Pope John Paul II, have been as critical of contemporary capitalist regimes as of the now diminishing communist regimes. This is hard for American Catholics to understand because anticommunism was for so long the glue that held patriotism and religious loyalties together. Communism was the enemy for both America and the Catholic Church; therefore, being against communism was being for what was different from communism. Because communism was, among other things, an economic order that allowed private ownership of consumer goods but was supposed to prevent the accumulation of capital (the means of production) in private hands, therefore its opposite was right. Its opposite is an order that defends the liberty of individuals to acquire and own private property even when it accumulates as capital and is used to create more wealth by employing other people and profiting from investment in their labor. This is a process that is inevitable in society. The issue is what kinds of restraints are placed by law on the increasingly uneven bargaining power between the owners of the capital and those whose labor yields the profits that increase the capital accumulation.

Catholic teaching since the twelfth century, though not before, has defended the right of private ownership. But it has never defended that right as absolute and without limitation. A general principle has been that God the Creator intends the resources of the earth for everyone. Therefore, those with enough wealth to live in luxury (whatever that is in a particular context) are obligated to share with those in need, and even those who are moderately comfortable are obligated to share with those in extreme need (which, at present, is an alarmingly large proportion of the world's population, and in many wealthy countries a scandalous proportion of the nation's own population). It is a distortion of church teaching to claim unlimited rights of private property. Yet many Christians are more influenced by classical economics that claims that unhampered competition is in the end best for everyone, recently popularized as the trickle down theory. If it were really the best for everyone, one could act on it with a clear conscience, but as it is demonstrably not the best for those with less bargaining power, what is often referred to as "the American way" really is in sharp tension with serious discipleship. The common assumption that people have a God-given right to whatever they can acquire without actually breaking the law is false. Restraint on accumulation of wealth by progressive taxation and other regulations is not an infringement of property rights, even if the progressive taxation is steep, as it is in most European countries. This is not properly a loss of liberty but an assurance that liberty is available also to those who are economically less competitive. But the tension between the values of "the American way" and the demands of discipleship can be very strong for many Americans who profit from the prevailing assumptions. One cannot simply equate "the American way" with Christian discipleship.

Chapter Eight

FAIRNESS AND COMPASSION

Related to the issues that arise in the tension between patriotism and discipleship are those that center on apparent conflicts between fairness and compassion. That life ought to be fair is such a common expectation that we seldom stop to reflect on what we mean when we say that something is or is not fair. The concept implies that there should be a certain parity among people or groups. One of the oldest examples is the punitive principle of "an eye for an eye and a tooth for a tooth." On this principle, one who kills another should forfeit his own life. One who steals or robs should be forced to make equal restitution. Originally, this was surely supposed to prevent endless feuds or reckless revenge by limiting the return of evil for evil to the amount of the original damage. Anyone who has seen playground fights has seen how easily violence escalates. And those who have become truly attentive to their own emotions will also know that anger is blind and needs to be restrained by reason, calling for a vigorous exercise of the virtue of temperance. Hence, the need for law to intervene and set limits.

Penal law, formulated in a calm atmosphere to cover a variety of possible cases, is usually somewhat better than a system to limit revenge. Drawing on the cumulative wisdom of the human community and concerned to promote the common good, penal law is best formulated as preventive and deterrent. The penalty should prevent the offender from repeating or continuing the offense, and it should deter others from embarking on this kind of behavior. Thus, it has been argued that the incorrigibly and drastically violent should incur the death penalty to prevent their being able to do more damage. However, many nations have already conceded that such prevention can be achieved by high security imprisonment, so the death penalty is not needed for this reason. Similarly, there has been an argument about deterrence, that is to say about deterring others from the same harmful action by demonstrating to them what the consequences would be. While the law is usually written in this reasoned way, public opinion often cries out for sheer vengeance, calling for the death penalty where the law does not impose it, wanting a more painful death inflicted than the prescribed mode of execution, wanting longer prison sentences and less prison amenities than provided, and so forth. The justification generally given for such cries for vengeance is that it is a matter of being fair to the victims of the crimes.

Such a sense of fairness raises the question of whether the victims or their surviving relatives and friends are actually any better off because of the suffering inflicted on the transgressor. The biblical theme of God's fairness or justice has a more constructive focus. By the justice or fairness of God, the lowly are to be lifted up to their full human dignity, the poor are to be filled with good things, prisoners are to be set free, refugees are to be brought home, the blind given sight, the lame enabled to walk, and so forth. It is true that the corollary of such readjustment of relationships is that those enjoying undue power, wealth, or privilege will lose these. However, what these privileged people are to lose are not the necessities of life but their disproportionate advantages. In any case, the focus is on the positive relief of suffering and betterment of conditions for those deprived. If we apply this to penal laws of our society, compensation of the victims by the guilty and by the whole society should be the first concern.

Prevention and deterrence are certainly valid and justified aims. But they raise questions, first about the real need or purpose of the death penalty, and then about what impact prisons actually have on the future of prisoners. Is it possible that while the public thirst for vengeance is slaked to some extent, the preventive and deterrent functions are not fulfilled? The kind of experience that many prisoners have does not help to refine their character or conscience or to equip them to earn an honest living or exercise responsible citizenship. More usually, prison has a dehumanizing and brutalizing effect, especially on the young. This raises some serious questions for conscientious people about prisons and their multiplication in some countries such as the United States. Communist "reeducation" camps in China and elsewhere may have been brutal in practice, but the basic idea was good: namely that the purpose of prison should be to make people better equipped to live peaceful and law-abiding lives in society.

Another context in which the idea of fairness is applied is in relation to property rights as already discussed in the previous chapter. In the United States, there is a prevailing sense that it is fair that people should own accumulated wealth, whether inherited or from the profits of their own initiatives, and that they should be able further to accumulate profit from investing their wealth in the labor of others. From a believer's perspective, there are important questions to be raised about this. The most obvious is about how and by whom the ratio is calculated that sets the relative value of the work and the capital investment. Should workers be paid half the profit (the surplus value created) or more or less? We know what the answer is in practice: unless a superior authority intervenes, the ratio is calculated by the measure of the balance of bargaining power between the participating parties. That is how wealth is increased in few hands. In poor countries with high unemployment and inadequate labor laws, for instance, international companies financed by foreign investors can bargain the workers down to mere subsistence or below. Is there a measure of what is fair, and how does one calculate it? Frequently in modern Western culture, there is an assumption that wealth and success in themselves indicate virtue and merit and should be rewarded, even if the wealth is simply inherited. It is an assumption that a believer is obliged to question.

A second question to be asked about the increase of wealth in private hands through accumulation of capital from employment of others is whether fairness requires a limit to the accumulation. In practice, the limitation of accumulation is always bitterly contested in the name of fairness, whether the limits are applied through systematic progressive taxation, or through death duties, or bluntly by confiscation as often happens in revolutions. In an abstract model, however, the cogency and urgency of the question become obvious. Though dealing with competing capitalists

rather than workers, the board game called Monopoly illus-
trates the dynamic: the player who begins with a small advantage and parlays it cleverly acquires progressively more
bargaining power until he or she is able to deprive the other
players of everything. According to the rules of the game,
this is fair play. But the game comes to an end, and in the
next round the players start from the beginning. The fun de-
rives from the fact that there is a combination of initial luck
and adroit management, much as in real life, but the nature
of the game is that it has no real consequences for the conditions of life for the players and their children and their
children's children. Even in the game, the chances are reas-
signed with each round of play. In real life, the starting opportunities are governed not only by inherited wealth or the
lack of it but also by educational and cultural opportunities,
by native intelligence and its early development, by various
components of health (which are closely related to economic status in childhood), by the contacts the other advantages offer, and so forth. If all of these factors are taken
into account, what is required by authentic fairness among
the people of any society?

Other aspects of human life in society that raise questions of fairness are such as educational and cultural opportunities. Is it fair that the rich can send their children to
the best schools while the poor have no choice? In earlier
centuries, this question would have been is it fair that the
rich can send their children to schools or provide them with
tutors while the children of the poor have no access to education? Because we no longer face that question in most
countries of the northern hemisphere, there is a prevailing
assumption that society is now giving everyone an equal opportunity. Research on what is actually happening challenges

this. In the United States, for instance, because of the way the population is distributed residentially and because of the consequent distribution of the tax base for state and local public resources, educational opportunities are very unequal, even if the difference in starting points for schoolchildren are not taken into account. Moreover, the job market is shifting toward more positions for the highly educated and less and less positions available for the minimally educated, whose other skills are not valued. These conditions place some very sharp challenges to the question of fairness in educational opportunity.

A further aspect of human society that cannot be ignored in the question of fairness among individuals and among populations is the question of health care—both large-scale public health provisions for whole populations and individual access to good doctors and health professionals. In public discourse in the Western industrial countries, there has been a declared tension between the obligation of fairness (justice) to all and the freedom of individuals to make their own choices. Many countries have resolved this by first providing an inclusive national system of health insurance coverage and then providing for some choices of doctors, health centers, hospitals, and ancillary services within the system. In the United States, there has been so much emphasis in the public rhetoric on the rights of individuals to choose that in this enormously wealthy country a high proportion of the population has no access to even basic health care. But the public rhetoric conceals the real players in the political wrangling over the issues— the large private health insurance companies and the politicians whose election campaigns these companies favor with their contributions. The questions this raises, therefore, concern not only the fairness of the relative availability of health care, but the fairness of the political system that decides such issues as availability of health care by the way political campaigns are financed. At this level, believers, and indeed all thoughtfully conscientious people, must ask some very important questions of fairness.

Most people in our society are at least vaguely aware of all the above. They are also concerned with fairness. Americans, especially, think of themselves as a people of equal opportunity, of fair play, of participation for all in the democratic process.

They see the United States as a place where immigrants who arrive poor, persecuted, and oppressed can become free, independent, and rich. Yet, in contemporary America, the "homeless, tempest tossed . . . the huddled masses longing to breathe free" are systematically excluded from immigration, and it is estimated that 80% of the farm workers of the country are undocumented immigrants with no rights, although the economy regularly and systematically depends on them and could not function without them. One is led to wonder then, how, with the national philosophy of freedom from oppression so widely proclaimed and professed, issues like those raised so far in this chapter are invisible to so many people whose consciences are not troubled by them. And these people include many good Christians, Catholics prominent among them. One reason surely is that questions of fair or unfair, just or unjust assume some criteria for what are the right relationships among people.

That is exactly what is not given within the cardinal virtues of prudence, justice, fortitude, and temperance. Good people are prudent: they choose right means to right goals according to their understanding of what the ultimate goal of human life should be. But how is this last determined? Good people are just: they deal fairly and are concerned with fair structures and dealings in their society according to their standards of what is owed to each and everyone. But how are they to derive an understanding of what is owed? In Western capitalist societies, there is a strong sense that what is owed to each is the right to compete freely for the goods available in the society. In societies closer to socialist principles, there is a prevailing sense that what is owed to everyone is a substantial safety net guaranteeing that basic needs are met. Good people are courageous: they face risk and conflict and are willing to take a stand on principle, disregarding cost to themselves. But how do they determine the principles that call for such a stance? Likewise, good people are temperate: they know how to exercise restraint not only in matters like food and drink, of anger and lust, but also when circumstances call for moderation in pushing economic, military, political, social, and other advantages.

Even for strictly individual issues, temperance needs to draw on criteria outside itself.

For large issues, local, national, and international, of restraint on the pursuit of power, wealth, military advantage, and cultural dominance, the criteria have to be drawn from a larger vision.

Biblical and Christian tradition suggests that questions of fairness are properly grounded in compassion. The relationship of the creator to creatures is entirely one of compassion because there is no possibility of proportion between creator and creatures. Anything that creatures can claim is entirely based on their need, not on their merit or their intrinsic rights. The godly quality that shapes human beings in the divine image has among its many facets the capacity for empathy and therefore the power of compassion that is at the peak of human creativity. Among creatures, what is owed to each is shaped by that person's need and by the ability of others to meet the need. Food and shelter, clean air and water, and protection against disease and the elements of the weather are basic human needs. Therefore, in fairness, society must supply these needs to the extent that it can, first to its own citizens and inhabitants and then to others in need, because these basic obligations do not end at national boundaries. They do not end at national boundaries because they are derived from our relationship to the creator as this plays out largely in our relationships to one another within the universe of creation. It is clear that the principle of free competition for resources meets opposition from the understanding that fairness is based on need. Competition for jobs cannot be translated into competition for the right to eat and to feed one's family. Economic competition for housing location cannot be translated into competition for clean air and unpolluted water.

When fairness is grounded in need, there are basic rights for all to eat and breathe clean air and drink clean water. No calculation of merit and no economic competition can do away with these.

But human need also includes productive participation in one's society and, therefore, education and training to the level that makes participation with dignity and respect possible in the actual circumstances of one's society. Hence, the concern with education. If the claim to education is based on need, not merit, then the best resources should be devoted to the neediest. This is sharply in conflict with the general assumption that the best resources should be given to those with greatest aptitude in learning or the greatest ability to pay. In fact, the grounding of our ideas of what is fair in need rather than in competitive achievement, or quantitative equality, or personal merit involves a reversal of many of the assumptions on which we act in practice and on which the priorities of our society are based. This is even more so when we extend educational needs beyond what is needed to be productive. The appreciation of beauty, the ability to enjoy cultural experiences of all kinds, and the possibility of personal artistic performance in visual, musical, literary, and dramatic works all belong to the range of experience to which the human spirit aspires, but these are areas of human life that tend to be carefully guarded privileges of elite groups.

If society were to respond to the need of the poor for beauty, of convicted criminals for encouragement and help in changing their ways, of the intellectually slow for excellent teachers, of the uninsured for equally good health care, and all sort of similar needs, this would establish a new set of standards for what is fair. It may seem like an impossible dream, but our Christian faith commits us to work toward it, and much in modern Catholic social teaching is based directly on this principle.

Chapter Nine

FAMILY AND SOCIAL RESPONSIBILITY

This question of how we decide what is fair, and how we reconcile our customary concepts of fairness with the divinely inspired principle of compassion, is constantly exemplified in the tensions between the pull of family and the challenge of social responsibility. Most people are aware of having to deal with all kinds of tensions concerning claims and responsibilities within the family. The concerns of this chapter, however, are the sharp tensions that often arise between perceived claims of family members and perceived claims of wider social responsibility. There are apparent conflicts of responsibility in terms of the way time is spent, the way money is spent, the expectations one has of one's own children compared with expectations one has of others, and so on.

For many people, and especially for mothers of families who also go out to work, the most evident of the tensions has to do with time. Most women who are the center of their households could easily spend their whole time and energy keeping the household and the family going, no matter what the number or shape of the family. Yet most in our time and society either need to go out to work, or think they need to, or want to because, except for wives of prominent public figures or the very wealthy, society bestows more respect on those who earn money. Some professional women and artists are so committed to their chosen fields that they cannot imagine not working in the field of their expertise at least part time. Yet these are just the fields that are so consuming that they are never really part time. The immediate and practical family claims are usually the most constant, demanding, and insistent for women. Small children must be fed on a regular schedule and tended and watched all the time around the clock. There can be no time gap, even of minutes, between a sitter going home and a parent being present.

The tension that a mother of young children feels between her home and work obligations is acute. Women are often teachers, physicians, social workers, counselors, and middle managers working in schedules where there is no leeway either on the professional or the family end. Our society multiplies tension and stress for such women and their dependents because the women are constantly trying to do the impossible. It is all too easy to fail on one end or the other or even on both. The virtues of prudence and justice come urgently into play in these situations, but so do fortitude and temperance. In the first place, it is necessary to have both the goals and the means in place. This often means hard choices about the kinds of work and the kinds of position that one can or cannot undertake at a particular phase of life. Unfortunately, our societal structures are such that poor women with limited qualifications frequently have little or no choice of the jobs they undertake. Their only remaining choice is often in the alliances they form with family members, neighbors, and friends for child care or after-school supervision. That this situation exists defines a social responsibility in justice for the more fortunate.

Once the job is undertaken, however, the individual still has to sort out the claims of justice between the job and the family. The tendency in our society is to see the claims of the job as nonnegotiable and the claims of family as having to yield except in direct emergencies or tragedies. This seems to be a function of the importance that money has in the societal values. The job brings in money, whereas raising children, caring for elderly relatives, and giving support to other family members is seen as unproductive. The values are skewed, of course, but they press on us very hard in contemporary society, so much so that we are likely to value ourselves by the same standards and to feel quite guilty when we spontaneously make the choices that put the claims of people above the claims of money. One must certainly do the job for which one is paid, but employers do not own their employees. They have not bought the persons; they have contracted for reasonable service from people who, being human, have multiple obligations and ties.

There is also the factor of power because employers have the power to dismiss workers who are not wholly committed to and maximally productive in their work. Sometimes, more in some fields than others, it requires considerable fortitude to withstand the expectation of being available at all times outside the agreed hours of work. Some employers and supervisors are so caught up in their own project that they act as though that project were the centerpiece around which all the systems of the world turn. From the point of view of the employer or supervisor, there are very serious considerations of justice in not subsuming the personal lives of workers into the project as though they were slaves in the literal sense. From the point of view of the employer and supervisor, and sometimes of the workers themselves, there is also a demand for temperance. For some people, it is easy to get so wrapped up in their work that they become deaf to all other obligations. Unfortunately, our society lauds this lopsided focus with its consequent injustices.

It is not only women who are subject to these stresses and tendencies to imbalance. In some ways, the pull on men to favor the job and neglect the family is stronger. Though this is beginning to change slowly in our time, society has less respect for men's obligations to their families beyond that of providing money. Everyone tends to assume that there will be a woman in the background who will have to cope if the man is swallowed whole by the job. Because of societal expectations, it takes more courage for men to resist the trend for the job to demand total surrender. And because competition for promotions may feature more prominently in men's working lives, in addition to the intrinsic interest of the job and the desire to do it well, there can be a considerable need for temperance in the investment in their work that men make. It is not unusual in our culture for men to feel that the best contribution they can make to their families is to work for promotions and to earn as much as possible. We have all had friends who worked themselves into a heart attack in their efforts to supply their families with more than necessary material benefits. This distortion of priorities can affect women also, but given the expectations that are pervasive in society, it is likely to hit men harder.

A believer needs to step back and evaluate these pressures. The family may need quality time with the husband and father at home far more than they need additional material benefits. This is true in spite of children who covet the most expensive version of everything with the most prestigious brand names and the newest releases in entertainment, all because of the advertising that drums on their attention from all sides. It requires considerable reflection and continuous attention from parents to discern what their children really need and how to arm them against the onslaughts of advertising and peer pressure. The parents who are most successful in this seem to be those who have been able to form strong alliances and community bonds with like-minded families. There is no doubt that the tensions between the consumer society and a Christian lifestyle are fierce and that our children are the pawns in the struggle.

Beyond the pressures of the job expectations and of the consumer society, there is another whole range of tensions that set social responsibility over against family ties, and here the churches are part of the tensions. For conscientious persons, Christians and others, the demands of neighborliness, of citizenship, of democracy, of social justice, charity, and peace have grown exponentially with the growth of communications, the globalization of economic activity, and the increasing complexity of commerce and finance. Most of us do not have the time, the specialized knowledge, or the channels to act decisively, effectively, and to the right purposes in the many affairs presented to us in the daily news. But we cannot escape the voluntary organizations, the churches, the political action groups, the committed friends. There are difficult choices to make. Without clear, well-thought out choices, one could be busy in good works every evening of the week and all weekend and so tired and discouraged that one is no longer able to distinguish when the busyness is effective and when it is a waste of time or simply inappropriate in the context of one's primary obligations. This takes a toll on family life and family relationships.

Unfortunately, this kind of busyness about good works of all sorts is also greatly admired in our activist society and even much praised by church leaders of the various denominations. The reason is obvious. Most of the good works do really improve life for people who need outside help or intervention. There are real needs to be met, real suffering to be alleviated, real issues of justice in society, and, in our times, a pressing need for peace building at many levels. To step into the breach is generous. It means sacrificing time and energy that could have been used for pleasure in sports, entertainment, social time with friends, taking care of one's own needs, or simply relaxation. But it also sacrifices time and energy that might have been spent with family.

And here there is not only the question of becoming worn out from over-involvement, and therefore a matter of temperance. There is also a question of justice.

To marry someone, to have children, even to set up a household with friends, is to enter into a covenant of mutual support and fellowship that involves more than money and household chores. It involves a real presence to one another, conversation, taking an interest in one another's lives and concerns, celebrating the good times, and standing by in the difficult times. This requires time together. The complexity of our contemporary society makes this difficult. People commute to work and school, and many people have irregular or unusual schedules. Almost everyone has all kinds of extracurricular activities. Many jobs require travel; some require unexpected overtime demands. In this context, time together in the family or household will not happen without special attention to it and planning for it. This covenant obligation has to be held in balance with other demands, even the demands of various good works and even when these demands come through one's church. The balance of justice involved is not always easy to recognize or to work out. When one has worked it out to the best of one's ability, one must nevertheless expect to be blamed and reproached, not only by others but perhaps also by one's own puzzled and struggling conscience.

There is good reason for this. It is a real issue. If all of us devoted our time and energies exclusively to our families, then charitable, social justice, and peace activities would not occur in society. Citizenship would be perfunctory, neighborliness almost nonexistent, and prophetic action, such as discussed in earlier chapters, simply would not happen. In the Catholic community, we have in the past had far too little lay involvement in good works of various kinds because we conveniently relegated charitable and prophetic activities to the congregations of vowed religious on the pretext that they had the calling to works of mercy and that they had no family obligations. With the explicit teaching of Vatican II on the vocation of the baptized, the laity, we have had to rethink those assumptions about active and passive roles in the church. Moreover, with the diminishing numbers of vowed religious, the vocation of the baptized has acquired practical urgency. We can no longer think of charitable and social justice activities as a kind of extra or elective activity for those to whom such matters appeal. Rather, they are of the very essence of the Christian vocation. Therefore, the call to be involved beyond one's gainful employment and family circle is essential to Christian discipleship.

That is why, in the struggle to do justice in balancing the demands, the need for fortitude and temperance comes in. For someone who has always tried not to shirk obligations and to respond generously to the needs of others, it is hard to say no to real needs and to justified appeals. It is particularly hard to refuse requests that come from one's own friends or from church representatives. It takes a certain degree of courage to refuse, although it is right to save time to spend with one's family. What makes it difficult is, among other factors, that there is no easy or clear standard for calculating how much time one should spend with the family or when. One does not want to be ungenerous. Moreover, for most of us, our own estimate of what is right for us to do is quite heavily dependent on the judgments that others reflect to us. But we have all had the experience that those who approach us to help are themselves so heavily invested in what they are doing that they see it as the most urgent and important cause to which we should all be attending. They cannot appreciate that there may be people appealing to us for help in a dozen other good works, each of whom sees his or her own project as the most important and urgent cause to be dealt with by people of conscience at this time.

How does one decide? How does one get the courage to refuse some of the appeals after one has decided? Three practices are recommended by wise people. The first is to give enough time to personal prayer in one's life that there is a calm space to order one's priorities. The second is to take advice from a wise friend who is not immediately involved in the matter. The third is to give every decision a little time before giving an answer to the request—perhaps a day, perhaps a week, depending on the extent of the involvement requested. Having done these things, one should then go ahead in peace of mind without worrying about what others say or think. This may take a lot of practice before the peace of mind really comes.

When all this has been said, there are some people whose temperaments and attractions lean in the direction of social action. The attractions range from the base and perverse to the sublime. At one end of the spectrum are those who must rebel and protest, and it does not matter very much what the cause may be. They will be in the thick of it. People like this became obstacles to the Civil Rights movement in the United States, to the anti-apartheid movement in South Africa, to every revolution that could have been peaceful but became a civil war, and ironically also in various peace movements, such as the movement in the United States against the Vietnam War. It is obviously an important call for temperance, to recognize and restrain free-floating urges to find a cause to champion. Others may want to get involved to gain acceptance or status or power, and there is probably a little of this in all of us. It needs to be watched. The love of power especially can make an addiction of social action, and in that case the family will certainly be neglected. But even those who engage in good works for predominantly good motives have been known to be so caught up in them that they fail to be aware of it when the family is neglected.

The tension between social responsibility and family responsibilities comes up also in relation to financial resources. The kind of people who are likely to be reading this book all recognize that they are enjoying far more of the world's resources than most of the people of the earth and that they have done nothing to deserve that. They know also that they are enjoying far more of the resources of their own country and nation than many of their compatriots who do backbreaking work for very long hours and who deserve far better than the share of resources that our economy allots to them. They know that the children of the poor do not deserve the deprivation in which they are raised. So the question arises at many levels as to what justice and compassion require when we choose between what material resources should go to the family and what should go to the needy. There is also, of course, always the question of how to direct and apportion gifts to the needy, but the concern of this chapter is the balance between one's own family and the needy beyond the family.

The first level at which the question arises is that of charitable giving. A simple Christian principle is to live frugally in proportion to one's circumstances and share what is saved. But this does not solve all the practical questions even for a solitary adult. It becomes far more difficult for spouses, parents, and people with other family dependents. In practice, both spouses must, at least in broad scope, agree on what stays in the family and what goes out to the needy. It helps, of course, to have thought this through early in life and therefore to have married someone like-minded, but many people are not in that position. Most people need constantly to work on a compromise between the spouse that has a more frugal estimate of what the family needs and the one who has a more substantial estimate. And this will apply to housing, residential location, vacations and travel, food and clothing, vehicles, and educational opportunities, not necessarily with the same spouse on the same end of the scale in each case. There can be no doubt that in a proper order of priority the quality of the marriage is worth some compromises in charitable donations.

It is more particularly in relation to one's children that the questions arise. As mentioned above, the children themselves are under fierce advertising and peer group pressures to want everything material and everything prestigious that is available in the society and to be deeply convinced that this is their right, which their parents are failing to satisfy. Advertising, as we know it in our culture, has gone far beyond information and invitation. It works quite insidiously to create discontent, especially in young people, to persuade them that they will not be respected by their peers and cannot be happy unless and until they possess whatever item is being advertised. It puts parents in the position of having to set limits at some point, so they may best think through on principle what is the right range or scale of possessions and then hold firm. In any case, they can expect battles. However, from the point of view of the parents' own discernment, this is the easy part of balancing charitable donations against discretionary spending for the family.

The difficult part relates to long-term planning, especially for rather wealthier families. More generous giving all along may mean less higher education funds and less prestigious schools. Or it may mean more student borrowing, with a burden of debt for the children later. Or again, charitable giving on a large scale may be in competition with trust funds for grandchildren. All this raises some incisive questions about what we think our own children deserve, simply because they are our children and were born into privilege, as balanced against the children of the poor in our cities, the children of our migrant farm workers, or children around the world who are starving, without health care, homeless, orphaned, or deprived of education. There is no pat or standard answer to this, but it is a burning question.

Biblical tradition put a numerical figure to it, with the idea of tithing, but for the rich tithing may not be enough for a conscientious balance.

Another level at which the question of this balance arises is at the political level. It is at the level of the kind of progressive tax schedules we support. And in the United States, it is in the kinds of tax shelters we do or do not support and the kinds of public programs we support for the poor. Most of the northern European countries have much steeper progressive tax rates and much greater benefits for the poor than the United States. The American argument has been that this is against individual freedom, does not encourage individual responsibility and hard work, gets people used to living on welfare, and so forth. The incisive question here is why we should find it so problematic to give the children of the poor a good start in life with benefits that we are very anxious to give our own children. Being children in both cases, they have done nothing to deserve a good start in life in either case. Their deserts are equal in the two cases and rest upon their need as children. Confronting this in the presence of God is a steep challenge.

Chapter Ten

AMBITION AND CONTEMPLATION

The reader may have expected this chapter to be called "Action and Contemplation." The reason for the title as it stands is that action and contemplation are not really mutually exclusive or oppositional categories. The monk digging and weeding vigorously in the vegetable garden may, in fact, be deep in contemplation with a text of praise from the liturgy of the hours singing in his head. The shepherd on the hills may be climbing tricky rock surfaces chasing after errant animals of his flock and yet be profoundly in tune with nature's God. Such contemplative attitude is, of course, more spontaneously likely in rural settings where the pace is slower and work is often less competitive. But there are many people who negotiate the morning rush hour traffic of big cities with their hearts and minds consciously in the presence of God. There are administrators of complex businesses and companies who negotiate their way through the activities and decisions of the day in habitual communion with the creator of all working in the world. All these testify plainly that contemplation and activity are not mutually exclusive.

However, there is truly an oppositional relationship between a mindset that is geared to predetermined or largely personal accomplishments and a contrasting mindset that has a receptive and responsive relationship to reality. The difference can be elusive, but it is real. Whether we recognize the difference in practice has far-reaching consequences. Discerning such difference in public life is an inescapable challenge for believers. It requires a habit of contemplation based on a high level of detachment and on a very disciplined search for the ascertainable truth of any situation. It requires a willingness to put truth above loyalties to party, race, class, and nation. Further, it requires a willingness at all times to discover that one may oneself have been wrong through prejudice or ignorance.

Very few people seem to attain that kind of detachment in public life and political careers, and those who do are generally made to suffer for it in one way or another. Yet even common sense demands such contemplative viewing of things as they really are as the minimum condition for justice and peace in human society. People of conscience know they must strive for it. People of faith know that the redemptive grace of God makes it possible. They also know that grace is not magic; it does not transform people without their cooperation and without real changes in their lives, plans, and relationships. Concentrated focus on predetermined goals of one's own, combined with determination to reach them at all costs, can effectively block the clarity of vision that might be obtained with redemptive grace.

What is at stake can most easily be recognized in some stark examples from the history of civilization. Most striking are those from warfare. In the first place, there are wars of the crusading kind: wars against the Canaanites in Hebrew history; Christian wars against the northern barbarians, later against the Arab Muslims (who themselves had carried out wars of expansion), later again Christian wars in the colonial expansions, and in the twentieth century against the communists (who themselves had also carried out wars of expansion), and around the turn of the century, thinly disguised, once again against the Muslim Arabs. What has been common in all of these wars has been the war-wagers' arrogant and unquestioning conviction of how the world ought to be—either how God wants the world to be, or how in the light of reason it ought to be. Practically, it does not make much difference whether the campaign is to establish the rights of the workers of the world, or to create a Christian civilization, or to establish Islam, or to eliminate communism, or to impose a "democratic system," or to engineer "regime change." None of these goals can be achieved by force. Wars to bring them about inflict horrendous needless suffering on huge numbers of people who are, for the most part, the poor and oppressed with little or nothing at stake in the outcome of the war.

The justification given for most wars, however, is defense against actual or threatened attack or redress of perceived injury or injustice. As discussed in earlier chapters, this argument is usually used to justify the violence on both sides of any war, thereby demonstrating the prejudiced basis for the argument. Such justification also assumes that the waging of a war is a demonstrably effective way to resolve the problem and that there is no less violent alternative available. The history of war refutes the first assumption, and the history of diplomacy refutes the second. A reduction of the argument for war to total absurdity was illustrated, for instance, in the second American war against

Iraq. The argument was that as the Iraqi regime posed an imminent danger, having weapons of mass destruction, it was necessary to attack the country. Had the accusation been true, attacking would have been a clear invitation to use such weapons. In the event, no such weapons were found but, like the war against Vietnam after the Gulf of Tonkin Resolution, the war proved to be one that could not attain either its unnecessary professed goal or its real goal of suppressing a hostile regime.

What are the forces that bring about such wars? One must allow the truth of the Marxist contention that there are always economic forces propelling the felt need to expand political power. But as Marxist theory has also claimed, the greed for economic expansion that fuels the hunger for more political power also finds ideological arguments to justify itself by appeal to higher authority, whether in religious faith or in "principles of reason." In religious terms, what is really happening is that we are confronting concupiscence and the darkening of the human intellect by "the lust of the flesh, the lust of the eyes, and the pride of life," to use a venerable formula. The impact of these is not less because we are looking at the actions of governments and nations rather than individuals; it is only much more complicated because of the complex patterns of decision making. The sinful heritage that makes it possible for human individuals to see situations distorted by greed, prejudice, and lust for revenge is multiplied and complicated in social situations. It is more complex because what is plainly sinful in an individual, as is killing for revenge or wealth, can be disguised in national policy as loyalty to one's country, protection of citizens, preventive strike to avert potential attack, and so forth. In individual relationships, one must oneself judge whether forceful action is justified. In the public actions of a nation such as war, every individual actor involved, from the simplest citizen or lowliest soldier to the one who holds the ultimate power to launch the war, is dependent on others for information and interpretation. The whole machinery of basically honest intelligence is often inextricably mixed with testimony and arguments of prejudiced and self-interested parties and their "spin doctors."

It is very difficult to disentangle the rights and wrongs, the truths and falsehoods in practice. No individual is equipped to do it. What is required is a large-scale collaboration of truly disinterested, well-informed, and highly competent people to study the situation, the claims, and the history. It must be said that since the mid-twentieth century, the Holy See of the Catholic Church has become more and more active in this endeavor and has employed more and more skilled and refined diplomatic resources. It must also be said that, especially in the United States, precisely the more conservative Catholic laity and those most concerned with doctrinal orthodoxy have been least willing to follow the guidance of this concentrated focus of the church's moral discernment on public issues related to peace. The perceptions and judgments of Vatican diplomats often challenge American self-interest and self-righteousness in economic and strategic affairs. They frequently question the economic structures and policies from which increasing numbers of American Catholics profit greatly. Yet because the Holy See no longer holds the economic or territorial political power that it once had, it is precisely in such political matters that its diplomatic corps is most able to be unprejudiced and see political realities as they really are. It is precisely in these matters that the judgment of the Holy See is most credible.

No doubt the reason good people are often deaf to such messages about peace is that none of us sees the world and its affairs with total objectivity. We look from where we are, and what we see is necessarily partial because it is seen from the particular angle of our own situation and experience. We can never be simply objective, but we can build bridges of empathy over to the experience and position of others. This is based on our common humanity. We all feel angry when attacked, fearful when threatened, shamed when humiliated, exhilarated when successful, and so forth. Because we have such feelings in analogous experiences, we are able by imagination to enter into the experience of others and know how they feel about those experiences. To do this requires a contemplative posture based on a detached look at what is happening. Only people of inner peace, such as is attained by prayer of a contemplative kind, are likely to be able to look this way and see what is really there. War and all kinds of violence ignore this possibility, and therefore expect responses from the other that are highly unlikely, if not impossible.

Thus, in the Palestinian conflict maintained by the long occupation, Israeli governments have acted on the supposition that ever harsher and more violent responses will stop the suicide bombings. On the other hand, the opposition has acted on the supposition that persistent and increasingly deadly suicide bombings will force the Israeli government to dismantle the settlements and end the occupation. Neither side has really imagined itself in the position of the other. Had they done so, they would have known that the effect of their action would be to harden the position of the others. Moreover, with such an exercise of the imagination they would have seen that the only way out of the deadlock would be by diplomacy. And, indeed, there have been individuals and groups who saw this clearly even in the heat of the violence. Unfortunately, it takes only one side, or a few parties, to start a war or a feud while it takes both sides, or all parties, to engage in effective diplomacy. The reason that diplomacy is always a better possibility is that it is essentially dependent on each understanding the position and claims of the other. It is essentially dependent on careful, attentive listening to the other and on imagining oneself in the position of the other in order to understand the response. Theoretically, this is also what a competent commander does in planning a military campaign, and in this context it may win the battle, though it does not solve the underlying grievance that caused the war. This must still be referred to diplomatic endeavors after the war is ended because the resolving of the grievance is a goal that cannot be reached by military means.

However, the tension between the realization of ambition and the contemplation of truth has many other applications. In essence, when people see reality in terms of their own ambitions, they are seeing it very selectively. When many people are doing this in the same arena of activity, they will clash, whether as individuals or interest groups or nations. In our world of many persons with self-defining and world-defining capabilities, community, peace, and freedom within social harmony are dependent on shaping a common vision and understanding in pursuing the social project. It is necessary to work toward the common good. This means, first of all, striving toward a true grasp of what constitutes the common good which, in turn, depends on an accurate perception of the situation in which we are. This applies to the human situation as a whole with its patterns of interdependence and its combinations of ineluctable facticity with unpredictable freedoms. But the same need to see the situation in its reality also applies to particular situations in which we are at any time, with their built-in restraints and their discoverable potentialities. This is what requires a contemplative attitude.

To cultivate such a contemplative attitude, the main requirement is detachment—that is, the willingness to set aside one's own desires, goals, fears, and dislikes in order to engage wholly in unbiased looking and seeing what is there. This is why contemplation is not really at odds with action, though, indeed, time spent in meditative silence will help to attain the necessary detachment. But contemplation is at odds with personal or communal ambition to achieve, to acquire, to gain control, or to be recognized. These activities create a focus of attention that is inimical to seeing what is really there, for instance, what others are seeing and experiencing, what the possibilities of a particular society are, and what the attitudes and expectations of those involved are.

For a politics of peace and justice, a politics of inclusion of all, nothing could be more important than such a contemplative attitude. It is much easier to acquire and maintain this attitude from some vantage points than from others. That is one reason, among others, that the political judgments of the Holy See, of the Dalai Lama, of the World Council of Churches, and of the leadership of the United Nations tend to have an attractive clarity and economy about them. They are in a position to look at the whole with a detachment not possible for governments that see their own national interest as the primary criterion for all assessments of world developments. It is perhaps most difficult for the leaders of powerful nations to look at world affairs contemplatively because they know and savor the seductive practical possibility of imposing their will at least temporarily on others. There may be a terrible cost in suffering for such imposition, but it will not ordinarily be borne by the powerful. These last can all too easily persuade themselves that the cause is just and that the suffering inflicted on the powerless is justified by the benefits it brings to the powerful, who choose to see it as the advance of human civilization. They may be able to persuade themselves that the imbalance of benefit and cost is somehow to be equated with the common good.

In general, power does not combine well with perception of truth because people tend not to risk mirroring reality back to the powerful. They fear retribution when the truth is not welcome. From a believer's point of view, local, national, and world affairs are seen truthfully when they are seen in the context of God's creating, calling, redeeming, and ruling all things. The obvious implications are that every issue must be seen in global context, in the context of both past and future, in the context of human dignity and solidarity, and in the context of basic moral values that are given, not humanly made. This calls for many changes in the way we understand and conduct public affairs. In the first place, it calls for a sense of community that is universal, global, and cross-cultural. In the second place, it calls for education and experiences in which more people of all nations actually get to know others from other languages, cultures, and political situations. Both of these are heavily dependent on education, both formal education in schools, colleges, and universities, and the informal education that people acquire through reading, traveling, and the media of mass communication.

Unfortunately, both formal education and the use of the media are highly susceptible to manipulation for political self-interest, sheer economic profit, and popular response based on various kinds of self-indulgence without concern for truth, goodness, or beauty. To see the world as it is, and to open up such vision to others certainly means critical evaluation and renewal of education and the media of mass communication. And that raises the question of who can undertake this. It raises the question of access in the first place, and that means that these spheres of activity can only be renewed by those who have not only the competence, the power, and position, but also the vision. What is called for to make human life in the twenty-first century more peaceful and just than it was in the twentieth century is a deep and widespread conversion to a more contemplative style of living in the sense here described.

Chapter Eleven

TRADITION AND CHANGE

Human beings create community, culture, governance, and economy largely by means of tradition. A process of trial and error, of experimentation and evaluation, produces customary ways of doing things. This is so in the most basic activities for survival, such as maintaining a water supply, food production, provision of shelter, and construction of clothing. It is also true in the shaping of language, the building of symbols, the establishing of canons of beauty, the accumulation of folklore, the recognition of patterns of relationship, and the emergence of titles that reinforce those patterns. Systems of government are brought about this way, as well as patterns of commerce and of the organizing of production and distribution. And it is especially in education and religion that tradition is given the greatest respect.

We know, of course, that there must always have been innovation and change, new discoveries, and new inventions. If not, we would not be living in the highly developed technological world of our times, with tall buildings and super highways, with motor, rail, and air transport, with machines that make machines that in turn produce things we use, and with electronic communication in all its dimensions. Yet even in technology, new inventions have regularly been ridiculed, opposed, and judged to be in some way morally evil or not to the advantage of the society. There is always a protest that it is not proper to change the way things are done, and at the heart of the protest there is usually the fact that someone's advantage or self-interest is challenged by the projected change. The law may be invoked to stop it, or the good order of society, or respect for private property, or even morality or religion. Yet technology is the easiest thing to change.

Often, however, there is an authentic and serious question as to whether the proposed change is truly an improvement and whether it is morally justified. This regularly requires the exercise of prudence and justice in the discernment and may require courage and temperance in the execution. For example, each stage of genetic manipulation, whether of crops or animals, has required careful evaluation of possible unknown factors that could constitute health or ecological hazards. It is all too easy for such evaluations to be tainted or suppressed by greed and self-interest that put the profit for the few ahead of the health of the many and the continued fertility of the land. An even more serious example arises with the possibility of cloning people, or producing them by artificial fertilization and implantation, and by surrogate motherhood. These are moral questions for individuals, but they are also questions with far-reaching consequences for whole societies, begging to be addressed by enforceable regulation.

Dealing with such questions does, of course, call for great exercise of prudence in considering all aspects of the proposed action and its foreseeable and unforeseeable consequences. It also requires attention to justice for all parties involved or affected. And the execution, whether of permitting or forbidding such innovations, certainly will always require fortitude and temperance, that is to say courage and restraint, to ensure that what is served is the common good and not partisan self-interest. But when all of this is said, there is still a gap. The four great cardinal virtues that make for a good and balanced life assume that we know what is right and for the common good. Such knowledge, however, has to be derived from elsewhere. We usually have the guidance of tradition, of the way things are habitually done because they have been worked out in the past. But proposals for significant and consequential changes carry their own new challenge. There needs to be a vision of the meaning and purpose of human life by which innovations can be responsibly scrutinized and judged.

Much is at stake in this challenge to articulate the meaning and purpose of life as a basis for judgment of new developments and policies. For Adolf Hitler's regime in Germany, the development of a master race of perfect people with certain genetic characteristics, and with space to expand and rule, was the overriding goal of human existence. In such a context, genetic experimentation with human beings and elimination of unsatisfactory individuals or whole ethnic groups at any stage of their lives as waste could be justified and might even be made to appear quite moral. This, of course, is extreme. But there are less extreme and more subtle forms of it. If the tacit assumption is made that human life is really only worthwhile where there are no serious genetic defects or seriously disabling conditions, then one can justify as compassionate the early elimination of those with such defects. If human life only has meaning at birth or as long as the parents desire the unborn child, then genetic manipulation and experimentation of all sorts, and the early elimination of the "undesirable," is rational and morally defensible.

What becomes evident in contemporary challenges concerning all the major bioethical issues that our society faces is that we do not have a national or international consensus in judging these issues because we do not have the necessary common foundation. Although the churches and other religious bodies formulate teachings on these specific issues from time to time, neither they nor anyone else can assume a common understanding of the meaning and purpose of human life. This level of reflection and understanding is not part of the public debate. The so-called Civil Religion does not help because it is designed to move things smoothly for those in power and privilege by appealing to the public self-interest of ordinary people. Without a better foundation in understanding the purpose of human existence, public debate over bioethical issues lacks direction. This makes any discussion of issues such as those just mentioned quite circular in argumentation. Certainly an Enlightenment type of philosophical foundation could be built for public discourse, but its foundational respect for human dignity and transcendence comes from the residue of the earlier religious tradition whose anthropology was grounded in its view of creator and creation. It was based on acknowledgement of certain absolutes beyond human willing.

In a postmodern context of questioning such absolutes, society is adrift when confronted with possibilities of radical manipulations of human life, and we are thrown back into some variation of Social Contract theory. This poses an enormous challenge to educated and thoughtful believers placed to influence the public affairs of their country and their world. We certainly have a basis in our long tradition of natural law for a coherent formulation of what is good to do in society in the great bioethical issues. However, we need to present this in vocabulary and in a style of argumentation that will be intelligible and persuasive in the public square of our time in our nation and eventually in the international sphere. It will need to be intelligible to the great mass of people to win public support, and it will need to be overwhelmingly persuasive to overcome heavily vested interests that run counter to the common good but especially run counter to the needs of the weakest in society. In the political arena, especially in the United States, these vested interests have great power because in large alliances they wield the money that heavily influences elections so that, at a consequential level, the political and economic powers are fused in very few hands. In the social arena, the large vested interests have great power because they have many ways to appeal to unexamined self-interest. In this context, faced with the challenge to persuade the people at large, any heavy-handed dogmatic campaign on life issues is counter-productive because dogmatism suggests lack of available persuasive argument that could be brought to bear on the issue.

In any change in society, there are tensions that soon become matters of moral discernment. But this is especially so when proposed social, economic, political, or cultural changes are called for. This is a reasonable tension. The whole point of there being traditions in place is that these are the tested and valued ways that the society does things.

One might say they "work." They are generally acknowledged as good and right and safe. Yet we cannot assume that all that is sanctioned by tradition is in fact right when seen in the light of God's rule of creation or even when seen by the rational principles of the Enlightenment. Looking back in history, we can see some things more clearly than we can see their parallels in our own time. It was, after all, tradition that African Americans went to the back of the bus and could not use public facilities. It was tradition that women could not vote and were not admitted to the professions. Those who began to oppose these traditional role limitations were both ridiculed and severely penalized both by public censure and by law, but they were prophets in their time. Prophets are always blamed because most people would rather hear that all is well with their society as it is. They do not want to hear that there are injustices, that there are people left out, and that the system is oppressive to some and ought to change. Those who benefit most by the prevailing imbalance will oppose change most vehemently, and they will also wield the most power in expressing their opposition. But ordinary people, even those with much to gain, will often be afraid of social change because they do not know how it will turn out or what else may have to change after the initial proposed change.

The true prophets are not always against some aspect of tradition. They may well be against some aspect of a societal change. From a believer's perspective, the wholesale legalization of abortion, for instance, is a far-reaching undermining of respect for human life, as is the legalization of euthanasia and any loosening of constitutional restraints on war powers. Yet this issue is matter for serious debate in the public square because there are many who are concerned about the liberation of women from having pregnancies forced upon them. They are overwhelmed by evidence of the extent to which women are bullied by men and forced into intercourse. Such people, therefore, are not appalled by the image of a "culture of death" (by abortion primarily) because what they see is "a culture of rape" (by forced pregnancies), and they see themselves as prophetic in wanting to overcome it. Similarly, they do not see the "culture of death" in legalizing euthanasia, for they are overwhelmed and horrified at the suffering that is inflicted on the dying by more and more invasive and manipulative medical ways of prolonging the dying process. This public debate calls for great prudence in working toward the greatest possible respect for the dignity of human beings. It also calls for justice in not imputing base motives to those who differ. One should rather try to understand what is the good that the opponents desire and strive to attain. This would provide ground to engage in dialogue about other ways of attaining it without sacrificing the good that one is trying to defend oneself. This, of course, calls for fortitude and temperance in continuing to be engaged in the face of accusations and misunderstandings and working patiently step by step to do what can be done by gaining sufficient consensus to act.

For Catholics, whether lay, clerical, or episcopal, the most intractable tensions between tradition and change arise within the church itself. The Catholic Church, hierarchically organized, is quite strongly and persistently resistant to change, and this does not always come from the highest authority in the official hierarchic structure. That there should be intense resistance to change is not in itself surprising because in a church setting tradition easily becomes identified with the sacred and with the will of God. We all recognize today, without thinking much about it, the fact that the church as we know it has changed constantly in the past. However, there is a sense that it must have been under the guidance of the Holy Spirit as it developed in the past, but that it may just be safer and better if nothing changes in our own time. Some go further and actually want to undo changes that have happened within living memory and return to what they perceive as the unchanging church of the Tridentine era. Until recently, Catholics generally, and those trained in theology in particular, were educated with very little sense of history and with little or no knowledge of the development that was always taking place in doctrine, in the sacramental system, in moral theology and teaching, and in church structures. While change in the Catholic Church has generally been slow, few if any changes were ever initiated without vehement resistance. There were usually attacks and accusations of infidelity, heresy, the beginning of schism, and so forth.

Many issues on which there is church teaching in place are also issues for the society at large. Catholics who are in positions of political, legal, medical, or other public responsibility often have specialized knowledge that church authorities lack. To fulfill their obligations responsibly, they may have to act against current church teaching. Many who profess to be ultra-orthodox Catholics have judged that they were entitled to do this concerning warfare in general and concerning the U.S. war of unprovoked aggression against Iraq in particular. They asserted this in spite of the contemporary strong and persistent voice of the Holy See and the U.S. bishops against that war. This seems largely to have been passed over in hierarchic reflections on what constitutes fidelity to the church. Matters similarly calling for prudence in acting on the available specialized knowledge constantly arise in the medical field, where change is constant and church teaching is resistant to change. Medical personnel and institutions face some very stark choices, as in the matter of maintaining vegetative life where brain function is authentically ended and beyond possibility of revival. An apparently traditional approach that did not require extraordinary means, but did require offering food and water, may by changes in technology come to look very different by the variety of ways nutrition can be forced into a body through channels not naturally designed for alimentation, causing horrendous damage, dysfunctions, and problems to various organs of that body.

Because new directives from Rome may ignore the changing technology, the extraordinary character of what is proposed, and the immense burden to all concerned, there is a serious ethical question about endlessly extending the dying process on account of a teaching that may be out of date and simplistic in present contexts. This is not a question of euthanasia, which is an intervention to end life, but a question of how far one ought to extend the dying process by artificially pumping water and nutrition into a body whose organs can no longer cope with digesting and processing it. There may be need of prophetic voices and prophetic actions to repeat the venerable axiom, "First, do no harm."

This applies, of course, not only to medical personnel but to all of us concerning instructions we leave in living wills and the decisions left to us by relatives concerning their deaths. Many Catholics feel very uneasy if they are not following literally what they perceive to be the traditional teaching in this matter. Catholic hospitals serve patients of all religious and ethical persuasions, and they employ similarly varied medical personnel. Their first obligation is to care for the sick with the best means at their disposal. Many Catholic hospitals are greatly burdened by any code that enforces undiscriminating forced feeding and hydration when their medical personnel, the living wills of the patients, and the pleas of the relatives all ask for more humane treatment of the dying by allowing the process of death to run its course with concern for such comfort as can be provided to the patient. Because of such tensions between teaching emerging from the Roman curia and the moral discernment of those closest to the situation, Catholics need to develop a strong sense of the role of personal conscience in making the right decision in the concrete case.

Another area in which resistance to change on the part of the Roman curia may have all manner of civic implications are some residual issues of church/state relationships. This, of course, has been an area of contention through the centuries. In a democracy it has some specific applications because it concerns all of us as voters and some of us as candidates for office and as elected representatives. We are called not only to decide whom to obey in cases of conflicting church and state authority. We are also called to take responsibility for the shaping and exercise of state authority. Inevitably, this will sometimes suggest that there need to be changes in the exercise of church authority. A key issue here is the extent to which central church authority or local bishops can tell voters or legislators what they are to do in respect to specific issues. This is very different from the question of when church authority may tell these people what to do in their private lives. In the public arena, change is continuous, and decisions must be carefully balanced in terms of all the factors. In a pluralistic society, both legislators and voters must take into account what can be done when the traditional values no longer hold. They must take into account what is right to do when the structure and dynamics of the economy change drastically. They must also take into account what is enforceable in the society, and this may change drastically also. These many dimensions mean that there is less black and white clarity; there are far more prudential decisions, and these need to adapt to changing contexts.

With great courage, associations of lay people in the United States have tackled change within the church administration called for by scandals in the church both in the United States and in several other parts of the world. This was by no means easy because the aura of the sacred tends to include all that is done by the hierarchy and the clergy. A church with such highly developed sacramental ritual and observance tends to inspire awe for all that is part of church functions and for all who perform them. Moreover, a church with such elaborately developed and centrally controlled governance patterns as are ours tends to blur the distinction between divine authority and hierarchic authority. It requires a very clear sense of the proper distinctions to demand of church authority to open the financial books. Even more is this the case in demanding that clerics who commit crimes be turned over to the civil authority. But these demands, in turn, lead inevitably to a demand that the governance structures of the church change to be more inclusive of voices of the faithful, to be more transparent, and to be more responsive to the pastoral situations in the local churches.

Perhaps the greatest resistance to change, in the name of hallowed traditions of the church, is the resistance to give genuine voice and influence to women. As roles of women in the postindustrial countries, and increasingly in other parts of the world, have expanded to include more fields of endeavor and more public and professional responsibility in those fields, the imbalance in leadership and responsibility within the church has become not only obvious but scandalous. The insistence of the Second Vatican Council on the responsibility of all the baptized for the transformation of human society has raised consciousness that all the laity have this vocation. It follows that all the laity are called to assume leadership in the shaping of society and in the shaping of the Christian endeavor in the world. Yet, in spite of efforts by local churches in many parts of the world to include women in roles of responsibility and decision-making, there have been constant small reversals from Rome of the freedom of the laity to assume active roles, just as there have been constant restraints on initiatives by the local churches.

These restraints affect women disproportionately. Because men can be ordained as priests, and even married men can now be ordained as permanent deacons and can preach, a variety of men's voices will always be heard. But we are deprived of women's voices and perspectives in preaching. We never hear the Gospels proclaimed in women's voices. The Roman restraints on initiatives of the local churches further affect women disproportionately. Because pastoral necessity has made the local churches far more open to change than is the Roman curia, which does not experience the pastoral necessity directly, initiatives to include women in decision-making and in proclamation of the good news arise more readily, and are more welcome, within the local churches. When these have less freedom to respond to pastoral needs, expanded participation by women is one of the casualties.

It is clear that there is scope for prophetic voices and prophetic changes within the church as well as within society at large. In retrospect, we honor prophetic figures like Catherine of Siena, Teresa of Avila, and many foundresses of religious orders who initiated changes in the roles that women might play in the church. In their lifetimes, many of these women were accused of imprudence, disrespect for authority, and much else. Change does not come without a price. At the same time, initiative for change in the church is perhaps where practice of all the cardinal virtues is most important and most difficult, and where a thorough formation of conscience is most needed.

Chapter Twelve

INSTITUTION AND COMMUNITY

The tension between institution and community is so pervasive in human lives and societies that we may not be conscious of it, just as we are not conscious most of the time that we are breathing or that the ground we stand on is holding us up. The most basic example of the tension is probably the family. Family is an institution by law and custom. There are legal rules for marriage, inheritance, responsibility for financial support of spouse and children, tax liability, joint ownership and claims for share of property, exclusivity of sexual relationship, registration of births and deaths, adoption of children, and so forth. Yet the reality is much more than the legal and customary structure. Family involves a sense of belonging, affection, closeness, a shared history, a web of personal relationships going far beyond the legally defined, and mutual responsibilities that grow out of the shared history and are unique to each family.

Community is so much more than institution, because community is life and the inner reality of relationships, while institution is basically a pattern of rules that are supposed to be a support to the life and the relationships. Because community is greater and more basic than institution, and because it is a living reality, it always strains to break through the boundaries of the institutional structure that is supposed to be supporting the community. This is what creates the tension. This is also what constitutes the challenge to discern in each case whether the boundaries ought to be maintained or whether they should be expanded or redrawn to accommodate the needs of the community. Though community is more basic in the order of experience and of human reality, institution is a need that all communities, even the simplest, have sooner or later. Even three people who form a club of some sort will have a purpose in mind that gives it structure. It may be as simple as meeting for breakfast on Saturday mornings, but they will need to set a time and place for their meetings. While all goes well, they will be unaware that they have put together an institution and are governed by rules. When one of them habitually comes later and later, the rules will have to be invoked and either changed or enforced. Otherwise the breakfast club will fall apart.

Something of this sort has been happening in our society with marriage and family. A generally agreed idea of the institution of family has been questioned in many ways by the intrusion of outside influences such as television, the worldwide web, e-mail, and so forth. While things went well, people barely realized that family meals together were an institutional structure that supported the community that is the family. When various extracurricular activities began to draw the children away at mealtimes, while round-the-clock work shifts kept one or other parent away, and the attractions of television exerted a pull to take one's plate in front of the "box," many people were simply puzzled that family life was not what it used to be. The more reflective knew that some structural elements needed to be replaced if community as such was not to collapse.

Something of the same challenge has risen in society in general, in education, and in churches, especially the Catholic Church because of the monumental changes that took place at and after the Second Vatican Council. In many aspects of human life together, firm institutional structures have given way to more permissive expectations of human behavior. Perhaps this has affected young people most, but eventually the young who grew up without firm structures of society become the older adults who bear most responsibility for the shaping of society. It is not only in Western postindustrialist society that the effect of this loosening of the supporting structures has made itself felt, but even more so in the highly traditional and elaborately structured societies of the Oriental nations. Around the world, there is the phenomenon of spontaneous aggression in more and more violently destructive actions, which we have come to group carelessly in categories such as terrorism, paramilitary activity, civil wars, gang violence, and the like. All of these are in some way the expression of a sense of not belonging, of a search for identity within community, of not having found the support of institutional structures.

As mentioned in the Introduction to this book, the twentieth century, while a time of vastly increased technological advances and of communication and collaboration, was a century of horrendous mass violence and of humanly produced mass suffering. Thoughtful, educated believers and other conscientious people were largely swept along, whether because they did not see themselves as responsible for public affairs, or because they kept quiet out of self-interest, or because they understood what was happening and thought they could not make a difference, or because they knew they could make a difference but lacked the courage to stand out. For most of us, the changes that happened were so radical and so overwhelming that we scarcely could rally the criteria to discern what to do, much less form the alliances to do it. To act requires community consensus at some level. But community consensus is not enough. There also need to be institutional supports for forging practical alliances and initiating action. In the twentieth century, traditional structures were already weakening, and powerful forces like Soviet and Maoist communism, the Nazi movement, and fascism attracted people who felt the lack of belonging in a lack of institutional supports for community.

In the twenty-first century, the challenge has been increased exponentially. With extensive migration of peoples, those fleeing for their lives or to find a livelihood, and those privileged people who bring their wanted skills and education to places where the living is materially more luxurious, social expectations are less certain. The culturally different are our immediate neighbors. Our children play in their houses and their children in ours. They bring their temples and mosques into our towns and observe different festivals and holy days. Their food appears on our grocery shelves, and some of them take our jobs because they are more skillful or work harder for longer hours or for less remuneration. Their children flood our schools, and it changes what the schools are able to do, in curriculum or in cultural assimilation to the accustomed civic expectations.

Around the world, certain Hollywood movies bring a vision, perhaps quite unrealistic, probably not edifying by anyone's ethical standards, of what the life of the materially privileged of the world is like. And around the world, certain movies from Bombay speak of a traditional society where everything is beautifully in place and there is a wonderful sense of belonging and being comfortable in one's identity. There is much that is helpful to the peoples of the world in globalization, but there is much that both impoverishes the less privileged further and at the same time arouses envy and anger over the felt exclusion from the good life.

We are faced with an immense challenge to create true community among the peoples of the world in the context of many established relationships that are not healthy, many cultural assumptions that are based on prejudice, many old wounds that still fester, and many old hatreds that have been kept alive century after century. Responding to the challenge calls for multiple efforts, in the first place at the basic human level of community relationships, and secondly but simultaneously at the institutional level. At the level of community, almost everyone can take immediate steps. For instance, in the world of our time, we of the West must all learn much more about Islam, its teachings and spirituality, its variety of traditions, its history, and especially the history of what Muslims have suffered from the so-called Christian West since the time of the Crusades. Another example is the need in the United States to know more about our Hispanic immigrants—the cultures and political contexts from which they come, and especially the economic situations that make many so desperate that they will risk illegal immigration and endure terrible working conditions under which no Americans would deign to work in order to send money home. Another example is to meet the homeless on our city streets and hear the stories of how they became homeless and what they experience while living without resources or places to go.

It is important to know these people and realize that they are like us and one with us in their humanity and their interdependence with us. But it is also important to learn what we can of the economic, military, and political systems that shape people's lives far beyond what they themselves can control. It is important to learn the history of invasions, conquests, and imperial domination that have made the poor nations poor and the economic conditions forced on them to keep them poor. Things will not change for the better in the world unless great numbers of people everywhere develop a greater sense of their interdependence and their oneness in destiny as earth dwellers. But especially those who are educated, who have some leisure and social or political power, need also to understand as much as possible the institutional workings and connections and power strategies of our world community. And beyond this we need alliances truly committed to the common good. These need to be large alliances, international and global alliances.

At the beginning of the twenty-first century, we have advantages that people did not have at the beginning of the twentieth century. We have inherited the United Nations, the Security Council, the World Health Organization, the International Court, the World Bank, the International Monetary Fund, all kinds of treaties already in place, and a plethora of collaborative bodies dealing with oceans and water supply, with the ecology of fishing and fish population protection, with ecology generally and the protection of forests and wetlands and threatened species, and much more. These are all institutional structures already in place to support and protect world community, and indeed to ensure the continuance of human life on the globe. The understanding on which such international institutions are built is that national institutions may at best work for the common good of the nation but are unlikely to work for the common good of the world population. The international institutions are expected to protect the common good of all, and on the whole they have done this. There is, of course, the constant difficulty that within the international organizations there will inevitably be lobbying and power brokering on behalf of the partisan interests of individual nations, especially the most powerful.

However, as successive recent popes have stressed, the United Nations and the subsidiary organizations are the best instruments that human wisdom and ingenuity has contrived to work toward world peace and justice and the common good of all. It is a terrible act of destruction, as Pope John Paul II and his diplomatic representatives vehemently asserted, when the most powerful country in the world rides roughshod over the deliberations of the United Nations to initiate a war of aggression to engineer a change of regime in a smaller country. This is especially the case when in addition to the slaughter and devastation of any war, there is no real possibility of any good outcome, and in the aftermath of the war a whole region of the world is destabilized, prompting the multiplication of terrorist networks across the globe. It is also an act of destruction, however, when the country with the most kill-power exempts itself from the authority of the International Court, unilaterally reverses treaties made for the common good, and in other ways acts to dismantle the institutions that are needed to support world community. Such arrogance of power hurtles the world back in history to a time when the structures to support world community did not exist.

What is true at the international level can also happen at the national level, when progressive tax structures that intend to be more inclusive of the less fortunate are dismantled recklessly to give a jolt to the economy by rewarding the wealthiest. To include the unfortunate in the benefits of the society is crucial to the nation as a community. The unemployed inner-city youths roaming the streets with guns in their possession, causing death and havoc and terrorizing the neighborhood, are the people who are not included, who do not feel they belong, who experience themselves as outlaws and aliens from the community of the nation. We need all the institutional structures that work to include them. It is certainly not a time in history to dismantle the structures that work to include the poor and disadvantaged. As much can be said about immigration laws, which are neither just nor advisable when they guarantee that four out of five agricultural laborers, on whom the economy rests, and who are therefore unobtrusively drawn to and kept in the country, are without rights or protection because they are undocumented and can therefore be hired below standard wages and conditions. In order that there be true community caring for and providing for the common good, institutional structures are needed that restrain the greed of the powerful.

The economy is not the only aspect of a society in which a tension between community and institution arises. The whole field of education and culture presents some important aspects of tension between community and institution. Customary structures of authority are often supported by titles of office and formal styles of address. In both East and West in the world, there has been a trend to become less formal about titles and forms of address, sometimes in the name of necessary efficiency and sometimes in the name of a friendlier community. It is clear that there are some gains in this, for instance in acknowledging the personal dignity of persons in subordinate positions and in diminishing temptations to arrogance and bullying. On the other hand, traditional titles and observances of courtesy and propriety have a role to play in supporting appropriate relationships. Perhaps the many scandals of sexual abuse of children and adolescents that came to light at the turn of the century would have been far less had there remained more formal explicit cultural norms about who touches whom, how, and in what circumstances. With the blending of many cultures, and the loosening of many of the "rules" for social behavior, neither adults nor young people had the institutional support to know with assurance how to conduct themselves in relationships that had a fiduciary quality and personal closeness. The other side of this is that with clearer social "rules," many innocent adults would have been spared the misery of accusations where the fantasies of the young people colored their perception of the intentions and actions of adults in situations of relative privacy. Even people who habitually act with prudence and with the justice that respects the sensitivity of the other can use the support of clear social norms in private encounters.

The tension between community and institution is especially sharp in the twenty-first century in the Catholic Church. Its worldwide extension and long history would in themselves make this inevitable. But the comprehensive centralization in an increasingly complex and fast-changing world add to this to the extent that one may expect ties to snap from time to time. Essentially, the church is the People of God, the community through history of the followers of Jesus Christ. As a community, it accommodates great variations in beliefs, practice, worship, aesthetic and ethical sensibilities, and much more. As a community, believers form friendships and collaborations, carry on joint apostolic ventures, share spirituality traditions, and so forth, often without attention to denominational boundaries. As institutions, the churches draw such denominational boundaries around themselves. Among most Protestant groups, the boundaries are rather porous. The boundaries of the Catholic Church as institution are historically tight and unyielding. Yet the official documents of the Second Vatican Council show a certain softening of the position. Those bishops at the Council who argued insistently about the reversal of Chapters 2 and 3 in *Lumen gentium*, the basic document on the nature and purpose of the church, saw with great clarity that a change they did not approve was implied by the placing of the community, the People of God, before the hierarchy, the institutional structure, in the document.

In the church as community, prophetic voices have free play, initiative comes from anyone, and change is the texture of the continuing work of the redemption. In the church as institution, certain supports are guaranteed, sacramental rites are in place, there is an established body of teaching. In these and other matters there is great concern for uniformity and for continuity, both of these last being reasons to resist change. In the church as institution, attention is therefore primarily to the past in the desire for continuity. In the church as community of the believers, the call to discipleship comes in ever various and ever changing circumstances that call for adaptation and innovation. Church as community, therefore, has its attention turned mainly to the future, in particular to the coming Reign of God. Issues tend to shape themselves differently for those whose attention is on the past and what it has established from the way they shape themselves for those whose attention is on the future and what new gifts it may yet hold in store.

The tension is inevitable and calls for recognition of what is beneficial in both aspects. Community, for instance, might well be stronger in the Catholic Church of our times if there had not been a lessening of the hold that the Sunday Mass obligation formerly had on Catholics. While it was seen as obligation, and therefore as an institutional constraint on one's conduct, Sunday Mass attendance nevertheless was what, practically speaking, created community. That is where people met and began to recognize one another as fellow Catholics, worshipped together, and heard the same Scriptures proclaimed. We may have privatized and individualized our Sunday Eucharists too much and celebrated community too little, but at least we were all there. To that extent, at least, this was an institutional structure that directly and effectively supported community. It is a challenge to the local churches in the parishes to capture both the habit of being there and the sense of acting freely out of personal conviction and commitment both to worship and to community with fellow worshippers.

Much of the time, the tension between community and institution in the church appears as a tension between the local church living, worshipping, and acting in its own cultural environment and the Roman curia issuing worldwide directives that do not respond to the actual needs and apostolic opportunities of the local churches. Catholics have perhaps been too accustomed in the past to assume that directives from the Roman curia should never be questioned because they were in effect the ruling of the Holy Father and because the merest hint of such a ruling was to be taken as the unquestionable will of God. With modern media and rapid communication, nothing in the world remains quite private, confidential, or secret. We have become increasingly aware of church politics, power struggles, national and cultural prejudices, all playing a role in the directives that come out from the Roman curia. We have become aware that not everything that emanates from the curia comes from the Holy Father, who is much too busy to attend to every issue that arises. In fact, many directives do not even come from the cardinals and archbishops at the heads of the congregations that are the departments of the large bureaucracy that is the Holy See. They may come from staff members who do not have the authority over the local bishops that they claim by putting the seal of the congregation on their letters.

What all this amounts to is a situation in which faithful Catholics, whether lay or clerical or episcopal, are called on by the vocation of their baptism to act with due respect for authority but also with great prudence, with justice toward all who are affected by a decision or action, with courage in facing consequences of their decisions and actions, and with appropriate temperance. Temperance needs to be exercised especially in the form of that humility that recognizes when one is being carried away by one's own arrogance rather than by the claims of the gospel.

Conclusion

THE CARDINAL VIRTUES IN A BELIEVER'S PUBLIC LIFE

The cardinal virtues are not the most central or basic Christian teaching about what constitutes a good life and leads to a profoundly fulfilled human existence. The so-called cardinal moral virtues are invoked in thinking through what is involved in the practical living out of what is central and primary. At the heart of the endeavor, Christian teaching about what constitutes a good life puts three virtues, called "theological" because they explicitly concern one's relationship to God. Language about faith, hope, and charity may all too easily suggest withdrawal from the world and from worldly affairs. In fact, faith is concerned with a constantly expanding interpretive vision of reality, which is a gift of God to those who are open to see what is divinely unfolded before them. The theological virtue of hope is the expectation, motivation, and striving that grows out of the faith vision. And charity is not love in the popular sense of attraction or emotion, but rather a total commitment of oneself, one's energies, loyalties, resources, and time.

Faith, hope, and charity have to do with how one understands the world and the meaning of human life in it, how one values people and possibilities, and how one acts in the world. Even when this is said and agreed, there is still a tendency to privatize and individualize one's understanding of what is involved. All Christians would agree that faith has to do with being open to God's self-revelation, but many think of this as apart from worldly affairs and having to do primarily with outcomes for human individuals beyond death. Similarly, many see hope as having to do with salvation of the individual beyond death, and charity as having to do with expressing one's love of God in one's personal lifestyle and one's love of neighbor primarily or entirely in one-to-one relationships.

Such individualizing of what is involved in the theological virtues seems to assume that the structures and relationships of society beyond the immediate level are not the business of the faithful believer. Such an attitude may be based on the assumption that public affairs are simply a given with which the believer as such has little to do. Or it may be based on the assumption that the way public affairs are governed and conducted is already a godly affair. The rhetoric of the Civil Religion subtly instills this assumption concerning the governance and public affairs of the United States. Yet again, the individualization of the theological virtues may rest on the assumption that the public affairs of the world are evil beyond possibility of redemption, so that the best the believer can do is to remain as much as possible untainted by them.

Official Catholic moral teaching has consistently denied all three of these assumptions, though specific directives emanating from church authorities have sometimes given a contrary impression. The basis on which Catholic teaching relates the theological virtues to action and participation in the public affairs of the society is in our understanding of our relationship as creatures to the creator. We are in the likeness of the divine creator in that we are in various subsidiary ways also creators. We modify what is given us in creation by our ingenuity and our work. We shape human society with its economies, its modified ecologies, its technology, its culture, its governance patterns, its access to production, its distribution of wealth, its laws and its expectations, and so forth. God does not make wars or make populations into refugees. God does not make treaty conditions, trading policies or trade barriers, national and international institutions, and restrictions on migration. God does not, therefore, make some rich and others poor, some countries powerful and others weak. Success in accumulating wealth is not a sign of God's especial blessing on rich families or powerful countries. It may instead signify God's anger (in biblical terms) because wealth and power have been acquired and are being used at the expense of the less powerful.

We human beings shape the world with the resources God gives us, and some people are in an advantageous position to press their group self-interest to the detriment of others. But we are called to work with God the creator and not against the divine purpose, and God's purpose certainly includes the participation and fulfillment of all. In a believer's perspective, taking all this into account, we must hold ourselves responsible to God and one another for the conduct of all human affairs according to the discernible will of the creator. But this is never simple, which is why in the course of the early centuries Christians adopted from their more cultured pagan contemporaries their distilled wisdom about what kinds of behavior make for a good person and a good society. And that distilled wisdom gave us the quartet of cardinal virtues: prudence, justice, fortitude, and temperance. Much thought of great minds and much experience of building Mediterranean city-states had gone into the reflections of these Greek philosophers. Their cardinal virtues all described personal character, all had to do with relationships, and in varying measure they had to do with city building, that is to say with the structures of society.

Characteristically, prudence is put first. The recognition of this virtue grows out of a stark realization that to live humanly, beyond the animal level of self-preservation, biological needs, and the pursuit of pleasure requires reflection about ends and means. It requires a person to be self-critical about behavior and relationships, and to act coherently and appropriately toward well-chosen goals. There is a logical step from this understanding to the realization that justice is a primary social need. For individuals to have the possibility of leading a prudent life in the sense just described, they require a society that has some stability and in which relationships are conducted on a basis of justice. Bargains must be kept, the law must be applied predictably, reasonable expectations must be respected, formal functions and relationships must be observed, and equality of claims within the recognized patterns of society must be honored. Such need for a just society indicates the need for just persons, that is to say persons who act and relate to others justly. Beyond this, the understanding emerges out of Greek wisdom that such a society functions only if its citizens are courageous and temperate. They need to be courageous in acting prudently and justly, beyond fear of danger, pain, shame, ostracism, death, and so forth, under all circumstances. They must be temperate in acting prudently and justly, beyond anger, revenge, greed, lust, pride, desire for pleasure, intoxication of power and conquest, and so on. There is deep wisdom in this Greek philosophical reflection. It will also be evident to anyone who thinks it through that this frame of four cardinal virtues calls for something more. It is not enough for individuals, groups, or nations to be reflective and self-critical and to act appropriately toward their goals. It is also necessary to have criteria by which to set those goals, and those criteria must derive from a vision of the meaning and purpose of all human life. One thing is quite clear: namely that as the Greek philosophers thought through the strategy of a good life in a good state, there were matters that did not trouble them but that would greatly trouble a thoughtful believer. These included the claims of enemies, the treatment of women, the fact of slavery, the power of death over one's own children, and much more. Another thing is quite clear: namely that all four of these examples and much more have not sufficiently troubled Christian states or Christian individuals over the centuries and in our own time, much to our shame.

Similarly, it is not enough for individuals or states or economic or cultural interest groups to act justly according to the established patterns of behavior and expectations of their society. The deeper question is whether those established patterns are indeed just, and this question cannot be answered by the established criteria within the culture because it is those criteria that need to be assessed. Any authority by which the criteria of justice are to be assessed must necessarily transcend the society and its members. It has to be at the source of all existence, in the authority of the creator of all, who orders and sustains. All religious traditions have reached toward this transcendent authority as ultimate arbiter of right and wrong, and most religious traditions show a strong convergence not in the symbols and rituals of their faith and worship, but in the practical conclusions of right and wrong in human behavior, both private and public. Such convergence does not come about without much reflection and debate.

In Christian understanding, the resources for that debate lie in the various ways that God's "will" is revealed to us. Looking at this from the receiving end of revelation, we are concerned with what can be read in nature, our own and that of the workings of the universe, the world's ecology, the behavior of animals, the possibilities for use of minerals and plants, and so forth. But we are also concerned with what is reflectively discerned in human conscience and consciousness. We are gifted with the power of empathy, that is to say of feeling our way by analogies into the experience of others, and we discern both kinship and mutual responsibility to support and not to inflict needless pain and suffering. We know what it is to be excluded, deprived, held in contempt, threatened, and wounded, and we know existentially that these are not conditions to be inflicted on others. Besides learning the "will" of God from nature and from the deeper levels of our own consciousness, we learn, of course, from experience and history, our own and that of others, and we are able to reflect and extrapolate from such experience.

To some extent, everyone is bound to be learning from these three sources. What is specific to the believer is the understanding that it is necessary to plumb these kinds of learning to their depth with reverence and with no exclusions based on self-interest and prejudice because what we learn from reality is the voice of God speaking to us with authority. What we also know as believers is how easy it is to see through lenses distorted by self-interest, prejudice, envy, revenge, arrogance, and so forth. This realization is expressed in Christian faith in terms of "original sin," a heritage of distortion running through the values, laws, and structures of society and through all human experience in each of our lives. Human freedom of self-expression and self-determination carries the risk of misuse, and there is a cumulative effect of misuse just as there is a cumulative effect of all the good things that have ever been done.

Christians, therefore, know that we are in a state of affairs both in private and in public life that continuously and inevitably calls for critical discernment and redemptive activity. And therefore, the task of discernment by the light of informed conscience is the most basic task not only for believers, but for all human beings. This is also the reason that the Catholic Church has built up over the centuries not only a moral theology that addresses itself immediately to the conscience of the individual but also a great and constantly growing tradition of social justice teaching. This teaching addresses itself to the criteria for assessing what is just in society and to the application of this in new circumstances, in developing economies and polities, and in increasingly complex networks of the world's affairs.

How Christians are able to adopt the Greek philosophical cardinal virtues of fortitude and temperance is also tempered by our understanding of our access to the authoritative voice of God. Fortitude is courage in the broad sense, both to do and to endure. It includes the patience to work for slow changes whose fruits may not be evident in one's own lifetime. It calls for willingness to take risks, bear injury and insult, and face death in pursuit of what is right, which usually means what is redemptive and prophetic in a world that resists such change. By the pagan Greek virtue, death to defend one's own honor or the honor of one's country is a laudable act of virtue even if it comes by suicide. Looked at by faith in the one God, the proposition calls for discernment whether we have in truth such authority over the disposition of our own lives or those of others, and even whether death and killing in defense of one's own country is justified by the end for which that country is calling men to fight. Throughout the twentieth century and into the twenty-first, there has been an immense outpouring of courage and self-sacrifice from hundreds of thousands of young men in the prime of their lives, who faced indescribable horrors and in many cases died in battle. Their virtuous courage is not in question. But looking over the history in retrospect, one must ask, "to what purpose?" There may be more true courage in refusing to fight and risking ignominy and blame as a coward.

Somewhat similarly, temperance as a virtue that expresses restraint in all that is not appropriate to the end begs the question of criteria for the goodness of ends. Temperance in food and drink and other things for athletic purposes is good while it maintains health and quite inappropriate if it destroys health even for the sake of a gold medal at the Olympics. It is inappropriate because in the order of creation, life and health are more valuable than high esteem or gold medals. In public life, temperance is called for in warfare at all levels of society. It is very easy to hold up patriotism in ways that foster hate and vengeance and bring about abuse of those seen as the enemy. Temperance is called for in the economy in the lives of ordinary people who may be destroying health and family happiness by overworking for the sake of increased income but at the cost of failing health and worsening temper. Even more is temperance called for by those who enrich themselves by investing in the labor of others when these others are not adequately rewarded. What needs to be restrained, in that case, is the lust after money, not even to spend but for its own sake, piling accumulation upon accumulation at the expense of whole populations that fall into grinding destitution. This is a very clear case in which the accepted standards of society do not stand scrutiny in the light of what we can discern that the transcendent Creator intends in the world.

These reflections and examples suggest that we can gain very widespread consensus in the public square about the cardinal virtues as a framework for a good human life and a good society and that, in itself, is already a good arena for debate on public issues. But it is also evident that it is not enough unless we can work toward progressive agreement on criteria for assessing what are good ends and good means in terms of the meaning and purpose of all human life on earth. At some levels, this agreement is not impossible to achieve because much that we say in religious language about morality and the common good can be said in language of a more common currency, because even the most secular Western societies have not entirely exhausted the moral capital of their religious heritage and, finally, because most religious traditions tend to converge extensively in issues of morality. Even the lacking element of the Greek philosophical discussion of the cardinal virtues, namely compassion beyond calculations of justice, still finds its place in public discourse.

Perhaps what can most distinctly be seen in the crises and tragedies of the twentieth century is the failure, especially of Christian believers, to look at public affairs at a depth of analysis that penetrates under the level of unexamined superficial conventional ideas of what is prudent (without asking for what ultimate end), what is just (without asking by what criteria drawn from what understanding of human life), what is courageous (without asking whether the cause is ultimately a true one), and what is properly temperate (without asking about the goals and nature of the restraints required).

What this seems to demand for the twenty-first century is vigorous Christian action. From the churches we need less flat do's and don'ts and far more help with adult conscience formation to be ready for new challenges and situations not yet charted. From the education of children we need less memorizing of answers and more exploring of questions. From all of us we need a great deal more effort in informing ourselves and in thinking issues through from the foundations in our faith.

INDEX

About the Author

Monika K. Hellwig holds a law degree and a post-graduate interdisciplinary diploma in the social sciences, both from Liverpool University, and a Ph.D. from the Catholic University of America in systematic theology and cultural anthropology. She also spent time at the University of Pennsylvania in graduate studies of the South Asian religious traditions. Long interested in the relationship of Christian theology with both world religions and the issues arising in world affairs, she is currently a senior fellow of the Woodstock Theological Center, was executive director and president of the Association of Catholic Colleges and Universities (USA) for nine years, and before that taught theology for three decades at Georgetown University, where she became the university's Landegger Professor of Theology. She is a past president of the Catholic Theological Society of America.

She has lectured extensively, nationally and internationally, and has authored thirteen books, coauthored others, and contributed many chapters and articles to journals and collections. Best known among her books are *Understanding Catholicism*, and *Guests of God: Stewards of Creation* and *The Eucharist and the Hunger of the World* (second edition, Sheed & Ward).

In private life she is the mother of three adopted children, Erica Hellwig Parker, Michael Hellwig, and Carlos Hellwig, and of three grandsons, Miles, Sterling and Quincy Hellwig.